AF564512

LIBRARY AUTOMATION AND NETWORKING

LIBRARY AUTOMATION AND NETWORKING

Dr. P. BALASUBRAMANIAN
M.A., M.L.I.Sc., M.Phil., PGDCA, PGDPR, Ph.D.
Deputy Librarian
Manonmaniam Sundaranar University
Tirunelveli (T.N.)

DEEP & DEEP PUBLICATIONS PVT. LTD.
F-159, Rajouri Garden, New Delhi - 110 027

LIBRARY AUTOMATION AND NETWORKING

ISBN 978-81-8450-347-0

Typeset by RAHUL COMPOSERS
358, Pocket-B, Phase-2, Sector-16B, Dwarka, New Delhi - 110 075

Printed in India at MAYUR ENTERPRISES
WZ Plot No. 3, Gujjar Market, Tihar Village, New Delhi - 110 018

Published by DEEP & DEEP PUBLICATIONS PVT. LTD.
F-159, Rajouri Garden, New Delhi - 110 027 • Phone : 25435369, 25440916
E-mail : ddpubs@gmail.com • ddpbooks@yahoo.co.in
Showroom :
2/13, Ansari Road, Daryaganj, New Delhi - 110 002 • Telefax : 23245122

Contents

Acknowledgements

The author feels extremely indebted to Dr. R.T. Sabapathi Mohan, Vice-Chancellor, Manonmaniam Sundaranar University, Tirunelveli and all the teaching and non-teaching staff members of the M.S. University for giving me constant encouragement for writing this book.

I also thank Dr. A. Rangaswamy, Professor, Management Studies, Infant Jesus College of Engineering, Thoothukudi for help and suggestions.

I would like to thank my beloved wife Mrs. B. Devi and my sweet children who shared my burden and helped me in many ways during the preparation of this book.

I would be a benefit killer if I do not acknowledge the services of Deep & Deep Publications Pvt. Ltd., New Delhi for their efforts in bringing out this book in a record time. Suggestions for further improvement of the book are most welcome.

DR. P. BALASUBRAMANIAN

1

Introduction

Information is now considered as an essential resource for all round development of the society. It provides tremendous opportunities to accelerate the pace of development both at national and international level.

Lucas defines information as "a set of organized procedure which, when executed, provides information to support decision-making. Information as tangible or intangible entity serves to reduce uncertainty about future state or event".

Saracevic etal., defines information system as "a type of communication system which selects, organizes, stores and disseminates the public knowledge for the purpose of communication of that knowledge to users".

Information is a key factor in day-to-day life. It can be considered as the lifeblood of communication and interaction. In a way, research is also a kind of collection of information from various sources and analyzing it to solve the problems or to satisfy the quest for knowledge. For a researcher, information is everything. A small piece of information costs a large to the researcher. The process of research is entirely dependent on information. Without proper information research cannot be started. From the selection of a research problem, till the printing of the report, information plays a significant role.

The researcher should have the ability to apply the knowledge to an existing situation or product leading to an innovation. This creative ability in the researcher depends, to some extent to which he is exposed to information on his subject. The information on his subject may be obtained from the following sources:

- Documents like Books, Periodicals, Technical papers, etc.
- Discussion with colleagues, and
- Attending seminars, conferences or similar meetings.

Information from these sources can help in the following activities:

- Selection of a suitable subject for research.
- Further specification or re-definition of the topic selected.
- Clarification of points.
- Substantiation of lines of work.
- Avoiding of duplication etc. Hence, organized information support is essential for research and development.

Some of the factors which calls for well organised information services are:

- The information explosion
- Lack of Time
- Interdisciplinary nature of subjects
- Scatter of Information
- Cost of documents
- Obsolescence of Knowledge

Library is an organization, which identifies selects, collects and process, stores and disseminates information at right time to the right person. The different types of libraries are public library, academic library and special library. Libraries have been looking forward for the better technologies even before the onset of the computers. The introduction of the typewriter into libraries was a revolutionary concept in late 1800's. Later stages of modernization witnessed the introduction of unit record equipment, the move of offline computerization, use of online systems, etc.

Now in information era, in order to avoid obsolescence of information a library professional should apply the advanced technologies to make his user community satisfied. One such application is library automation.

Enabling technologies, resulted in moving libraries and information centers into the computer age. The first part of this automation process was computerization of the circulation system which was perceived as a real need. A move towards authority retrieval and thereafter the catalogue card followed a few years later. Meanwhile, work had been underway in information retrieval in the database and online world.

Previously, libraries had to depend largely on their own staff to prepare in-house catalogue cards. The need for standardization, even in the manual age, led to AACR2 [Anglo-American Cataloguing Rules 2], and later to the ISBD [International Standard for Book Description] format. Computerization of these bibliographic descriptions led to a further requirement for standards of bibliographic descriptions for Machine-Readable Catalogue formats (MARC). This requirement was borne for an "exchange" medium for bibliographic data.

NEED AND PURPOSES OF COMPUTERISATION

Computerisation initially took place in large libraries for management convenience. A centrally located store of bibliographic records in machine readable format could be used as a resource by many libraries.

Library automation systems became firmly established and recognized as a beneficial technology for the librarian. As computer power increased with a reduction in its prices, the automation providers increased the scope of the library automation functions. This led to the integrated library management system (ILS). These systems enable library staff to perform almost all of their functions "on-line", often meaning that data entered in one part of an integrated system can be used again elsewhere, thus saving time and money and further ensuring accuracy.

A typical ILS system provides a cataloguing module, OPAC, circulation control module, purchasing module, serials management module, import module and reports module. Others may also include facilities for inter-library loans.

IMPROVEMENT OVER COMPUTERISED ENVIRONMENT

As the technology advanced, so did the library automation systems. The main focus was on improving the ability for the borrower to retrieve information from the library automation system. Command driven retrieval was replaced by menu-driven retrieval. OPAC terminals were set-up in libraries with options to perform simplified search strategies. The majority of systems were either on mainframe computers or on vendor specific hardware. Access to the database was through an OPAC terminal in the library.

The next advance was to enable desktop computer users access to the library over the organization-wide network. This meant that querying of the library database could be done remotely. Hitherto libraries had been running (and in some cases still are running) a suite of electronic online services for their patrons. There was access to the local catalogue. Online service provision was accessible by trained information scientists. Subject specialist libraries would often have a CD-ROM terminal set-up to enable users to perform more specific content searches.

The point is, that all of these services were in almost all cases being offered from different points of access. In fact, it has proved to be the system departments that have indirectly led to changes in the way the technology has affected libraries. Technology-led solutions gradually became popular and got widely used.

Librarians have not been slow to react to the enormous potential of the Internet as resource provider. Above all librarians, like any other professionals, have to justify their service to their management in terms of quality and cost. Managing a library is no more about handling printed materials only.

Users are becoming much more demanding and sophisticated in their requirements. They require information in machine readable format, they require to access video information, sound, all sorts of digitized media.

Terms such as Electronic Library, Digital Library and Virtual Library, were defined separately in isolated compartments. Today, the technological advancements have made all three concepts more or less the same. Americans have popularized the term digital library to denote all the three concepts. Electronic Library is the first topic in the syllabus for this paper. In the lesson package, the term "Digital Library" and "Electronic Library" are used interchangeably.

2

Communication

The word communication comes from the Latin word "Communicare" meaning to talk together, confer, discourse and consult with one another. Through communication one can share knowledge, information and experience, and thus understand, persuade, convert or control their fellows. Thus communication is the process of exchanging information and ideas. An active process, it involves encoding, transmitting, and decoding intended messages. There are many means of communicating and many different language systems. Speech and language are only a portion of communication. Other aspects of communication may enhance or even eclipse the linguistic code.

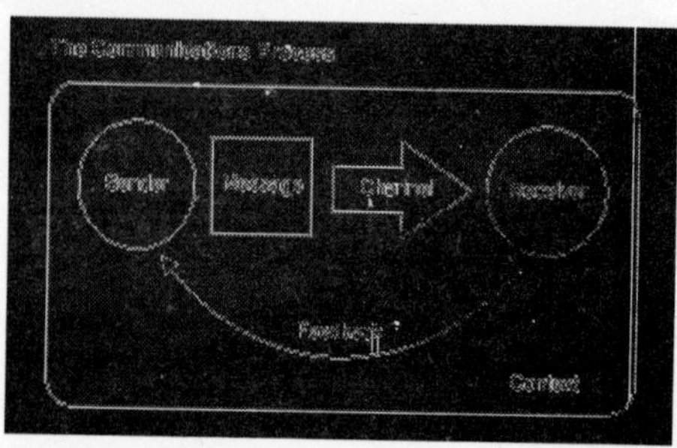

Communication is the process of sharing information. In a simplistic form information is sent from a sender or encoder to a receiver or decoder. In a more complex form feedback links a sender to a receiver. This requires a symbolic activity, sometimes via a language.

Specialised fields focus on various aspects of communication and include :

- Mass Communication,
- Communication Studies,
- Organizational Communication,
- Sociolinguistics,
- Conversation Analysis,
- Cognitive Linguistics,
- Linguistics,
- Pragmatics,
- Semiotics, and
- Discourse Analysis

Communication as a named and unified discipline has a history of contestation that goes back to the Socratic dialogues, in many ways making it the first and most contestatory of all early sciences and philosophies. There are many definitions for the term communication. Some definitions are broad, recognizing that animals can communicate, and some are more narrow, only including human beings within the parameters of human symbolic interaction.

Nonetheless, communication is usually described along three major dimensions

1. content,
2. form, and
3. destination

With the presence of "communication noise" these three components of communication often become skewed and inaccurate. Between parties, communication content includes acts that declare knowledge and experiences, give advice and commands, and ask questions. These acts may take many forms, including gestures (non-verbal communication, sign language and body language), writing, or verbal speaking. The form depends on the symbol systems used. Together, communication content and form make messages that are sent towards a destination. The target can be oneself, another person (in interpersonal communication), or another entity (such as a corporation or group).

COMMUNICATION MEDIA

The beginning of human communication through artificial channels, i.e. not *vocalization* or gestures, goes back to ancient *cave paintings*, drawn maps, and *writing*. Our indebtedness to the *Ancient Romans* in the field of communication does not end with the Latin root "communicare". They devised what might be described as the first real mail or *postal system* in order to centralize control of the *empire* from *Rome*. This allowed for *personal letters* and for Rome to gather knowledge about events in its many widespread provinces.

In the last century, a revolution in *telecommunications* has greatly altered communication by providing new media for long distance communication. The first transatlantic two-way *radio* broadcast occurred on *July 25, 1920* and led to common communication via analogue and digital media:

Analog telecommunications include traditional *Telephony*, *radio*, and *TV* broadcasts.

Digital telecommunications allow for *computer-mediated communication*, *telegraphy*, and *computer networks*.

Communications media impact more than the reach of messages. They impact content and customs; for example, *Thomas Edison* had to discover that hello was the least ambiguous greeting by voice over a distance; previous greetings such as hail tended to be garbled in the transmission. Similarly, the terseness of *e-mail* and *chat rooms* produced the need for the *emotion*.

Modern communication media now allow for intense long-distance exchanges between larger number of people (many-to-many communication via *e-mail*, *Internet forums*). On the other hand, many traditional broadcast media and mass media favor one-to-many communication *(television, cinema,* radio, newspaper, magazines).

The adoption of a dominant communication medium is important enough that historians have folded civilization into "ages" according to the medium most widely used. A book titled "Five Epochs of Civilization" by William McGaughey (Thistlerose, 2000) divides history into the following stages: Ideographic writing produced the first civilization; alphabetic writing, the second; printing, the third; electronic recording and broadcasting, the fourth; and computer communication, the fifth.

While it could be argued that these "Epochs" are just a historian's construction, digital and computer communication shows concrete evidence of changing the way humans organize. The latest *trend* in communication, termed *smart mobbing,* involves *ad-hoc* organization through mobile devices, allowing for effective many-to-many communication and *social networking.*

COMMUNICATION THEORY

We might say that *communication* consists of *transmitting information* from one person to another. In fact, many scholars of communication take this as a *working definition,* and use *Lasswell's* maxim ("who says what to whom in what channel with what effect") as a means of circumscribing the field of communication theory. In those respects *information theory* largely covers the domain of communication theory. Others suggest that a ritual process of communication exists, one that cannot be artificially abstracted from a particular historical and social context. Thus, communication remains an ill-defined concept, and while we may casually use the word with some frequency, it remains difficult to arrive at a precise definition agreeable to most of those who consider themselves communication scholars.

Another formal approach to understanding communication in groups is the Multiagent Communication Theory developed by Eric Werner. Werner's theory extends Shannon's information theory by including the representational states of the agent (actor, sender or receiver). These representational states include intentional state, the information state and the evaluative and emotive state of the agent. By including these states the theory is able to describe communication in social processes that involve cooperation between groups of agents. The theory is also able to describe hierarchies of social systems of agents in communicative networks.

Communication stands so deeply rooted in human behaviors and the structures of society that scholars have difficulty thinking of it while excluding social or behavioral events. Since communication theory remains a relatively young field of inquiry, one probably cannot yet expect a conceptualization of communication which all or most of those who work in the area would share.

COMMUNICATION MODELS

A very well-known model of communication was developed by Shannon and Weaver (1949), as the prototypical example of a transmissive model of communication. This model reduces communication to a process of 'transmitting information'. The underlying metaphor of communication as transmission underlies 'commonsense' everyday usage but is in many ways misleading and repays critical attention.

Shannon and Weaver's model is one which is widely accepted as one of the main seeds out of which Communication Studies has grown. Claude Shannon and Warren Weaver were not social scientists but engineers working for Bell Telephone Labs in the United States. Their goal was to ensure the maximum efficiency of telephone cables and radio waves. They developed a model of communication, which was intended to assist in developing a mathematical theory of communication. Shannon and Weaver's work proved valuable for communication engineers in dealing with such issues as the capacity of various communication channels in 'bits per second'. It contributed to computer science. It led to very useful work on redundancy in language. And in making 'information' 'measurable' it gave birth to the mathematical study of 'information theory'. However, these directions are not our concern here. The problem is that some commentators have claimed that Shannon and Weaver's model has a much wider application to human communication than a purely technical one.

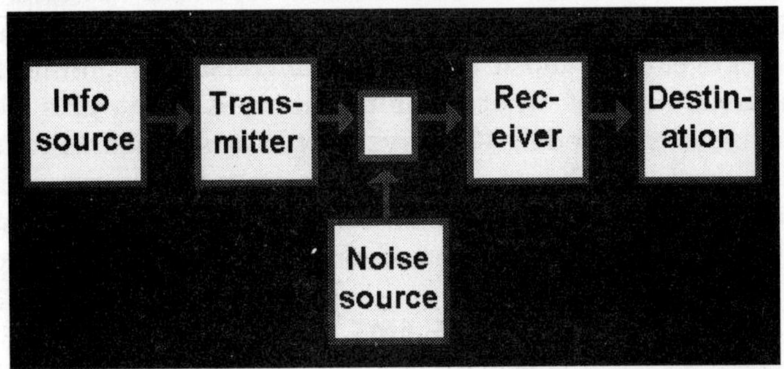

C & W's Original Model Consisted of Five Elements

- An information source, which produces a message.
- A transmitter, which encodes the message into signals.
- A channel, to which signals are adapted for transmission.
- A receiver, which 'decodes' (reconstructs) the message from the signal.
- A destination, where the message arrives.

A sixth element, noise is a dysfunctional factor: any interference with the message traveling along the channel (such as 'static' on the telephone or radio), which may lead to the signal, received being different from that sent.

For the telephone the channel is a wire, the signal is an electrical current in it, and the transmitter and receiver are the telephone handsets. Noise would include crackling from the wire. In conversation, my mouth is the transmitter, the signal is the sound waves, and your ear is the receiver. Noise would include any distraction.

Although in Shannon and Weaver's model a speaker and a listener would strictly be the source and the destination rather than the transmitter and the receiver, in discussions of the model the participants are commonly humanised as the sender and the receiver. Shannon and Weaver's transmission model is the best-known example of the 'informational' approach to communication. Although no serious communication theorist would still accept it, it has also been the most influential model of communication, which has yet been developed, and it reflects a commonsense (if misleading) understanding of what communication is. Lasswell's verbal version of this model: '*Who* says *what* in *which* channel to *whom* with *what effect*?' was reflected in subsequent research in human communication which was closely allied to behaviouristic approaches.

LEVELS OF PROBLEMS IN THE ANALYSIS OF COMMUNICATION

Shannon and Weaver argued that there were three levels of problems of communication :

- *The technical problem*: how accurately can the message be transmitted?
- *The semantic problem*: how precisely is the meaning 'conveyed'?
- *The effectiveness problem*: how effectively does the received meaning affect behaviour?

Shannon and Weaver somewhat naively assumed that sorting out Level A problems would lead to improvements at the other levels.

Although the concept of 'noise' does make some allowance for the way in which messages may be 'distorted', this frames the issue in terms of incidental 'interference' with the sender's intentions rather than in terms of a central and purposive process of interpretation. The concept reflects Shannon and Weaver's concern with accuracy and efficiency.

WEAKNESSES OF THE TRANSMISSION MODEL OF COMMUNICATION

The transmission model is not merely a gross oversimplification but a dangerously misleading misrepresentation of the nature of human communication. This is particularly important since it underlies the 'commonsense' understanding of what communication is. Whilst such usage may be adequate for many everyday purposes, in the context of the study of media and communication the concept needs critical reframing.

SCIENTIFIC COMMUNICATION CHANNELS

Scientific information can be communicated in a number of different ways:

- Formal printed channels
- Oral channels
- Electronic mail and electronic conferences

FORMAL PRINTED CHANNELS

Scholarly communication normally leads to some type of formal publication (making public) results, findings, observations and views arising from the researcher's work. Traditionally these have taken the form of printed material. Libraries aim to acquire, register and store printed and other media of this formal type, thereby providing scholars with access to past work (or a portion of it).

THE ADVANTAGES OF THE FORMAL PRINTED CHANNELS ARE THAT

1. Information can be spread to a widely scattered group of readers.
2. Detailed information, such as descriptions of methods, tables, diagrams, results, etc., can easily be given.
3. Printed documents contain information which can be critically examined and verified.
4. The documents can easily be referred to as, and when required.

5. Published documents provide a means for establishing the "priority" of academic work, and thereby contribute to establishing academic merit for the author(s).

ORAL CHANNELS

Traditionally, the main forms of informal communication in science, technology, medicine, etc. have been through verbal communication channels—personal contacts with colleagues and teachers—seminars, lectures, and discussions at conferences, fairs etc.

The Advantages of Oral Channels of Communication

- Are fast-useful for obtaining very recent unpublished information.
- Are based on two-way communication and therefore promote an understanding of the real information need(s) and the communication of relevant information.
- Are flexible.
- Simplify and facilitate the transmission of information between people working in different subject areas (useful in interdisciplinary studies).
- Are easy and pleasant to use.

The Disadvantages of Oral Channels of Communication

- Are not open to everyone-established researchers have access to good networks of contacts, but these usually take time to cultivate.
- Can lead to misconceptions because the information is sometimes incomplete (lack of detail etc.).
- Are difficult to maintain and therefore unstable.

ELECTRONIC MAIL AND ELECTRONIC CONFERENCES

The Internet can be used for Electronic mail or E-mail,

which is a hybrid between informal and formal communication. This gives a rapid and relatively inexpensive method of direct communication between people or groups of people. E-mail has a number of advantages:

- Communication is independent of global time differences.
- Communication can take place even without the receiver having to be in place (contrast the telephone).
- It is easy to transmit text documents.
- Mail can be printed and stored if required.

The network can be used to provide electronic conferencing facilities between users interested in a specific field or topic. This allows the user to exchange news and views and to seek advice from other with similar interests. An example of such a conferencing system is the USENET.

COMMUNICATION AND MEDIA

Telecommunication means sending information in any form from one place to another using electronic or light emitting media. Data communication is a more specific term. It describes the transmitting and receiving of data over communication links. It may comprise one or more computer systems and a variety of input/output terminals. Many forms of telecommunications now rely heavily on computers and computerised devices. Generally a communications network is any arrangement where a sender transmits a message to a receiver over a channel consisting of some type of medium.

TERMINALS

Terminals include video display terminals and other end user workstations. Any input/output device that uses a network to transmit or receive data is a terminal. This includes microcomputers, telephones, fax machines, etc.

TELECOMMUNICATION PROCESSORS

These are devices, which support data transmission and reception between terminals and computers. These devices such as modems, multiplexers and front-end processors, perform a variety of control and support functions in a network. For example, they convert data from digital to analog and back, code and decode data, and control accuracy and efficiency of the flow of data between computers and terminals in a network.

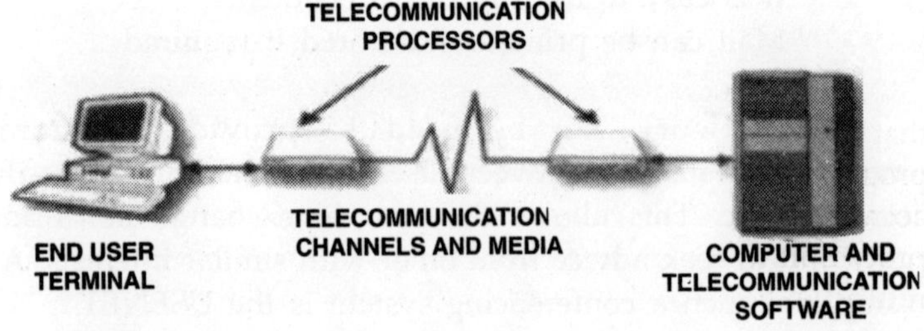

COMPONENTS OF COMMUNICATION NETWORK

Telecommunication Channels and Media

The media over which data are transmitted and received are called telecommunication channels. Telecommunication channels use combinations of media, such as copper wires, coaxial cables, fiber optic cables, microwave systems and communication sat systems to interconnect the other components of a network.

COMPUTER NETWORKS

Networks interconnect computers of all sizes and types so that they can carry out their information processing assignments. For example, a mainframe computer may serve as a host computer for a large organization's network, assisted by minicomputers acting as network servers for smaller networks of end user microcomputer workstations.

TELECOMMUNICATION SOFTWARE

Telecommunication software consists of programs that reside in host computer systems, communication control computers and end user computers. This controls the telecommunication activities of the computer systems and manage the functions networks.

No matter how large and complex the real world networks may appear to be, these five basic categories of components must be at work to support a network.

COMMUNICATION PROCESSORS

Communication processors resemble computer CPUs in that they have similar circuitry, have memories, and can be programmed, but their purpose is limited—to enhance data communications between two points. Communication processors include the following: modems, message switchers, multiplexers, concentrators and controllers, and front-end processors.

MODEMS

The Modem has been coined with two English words Modulator Demodulator. Modems are the most common type of communication processors. They convert the digital signals from a computer or transmission terminal at one end of a communication link into analog signals, which can be transmitted over ordinary telephone lines.

A modem at the other end of the communication line converts the transmitted data back into digital form at the receiving terminal. The process is known as modulation and demodulation, and the word modem is a combined abbreviation of those two words. Modems come in several forms including small stand-alone units, plug-in circuit boards, and microelectronic modem chips.

Modems are necessary because ordinary telephone lines are primarily designed to handle continuous analog signals, such as the human voice. Since data transmissions from computers are in digital form, devices are necessary to convert digital signals into appropriate analog transmission frequencies, and *vice-versa*.

MESSAGE SWITCHERS

A message switcher is a processor that receives data messages from terminals, determines their destination, and routes them one at a time to the CPU. It distributes the messages coming from the CPU to the appropriate terminal.

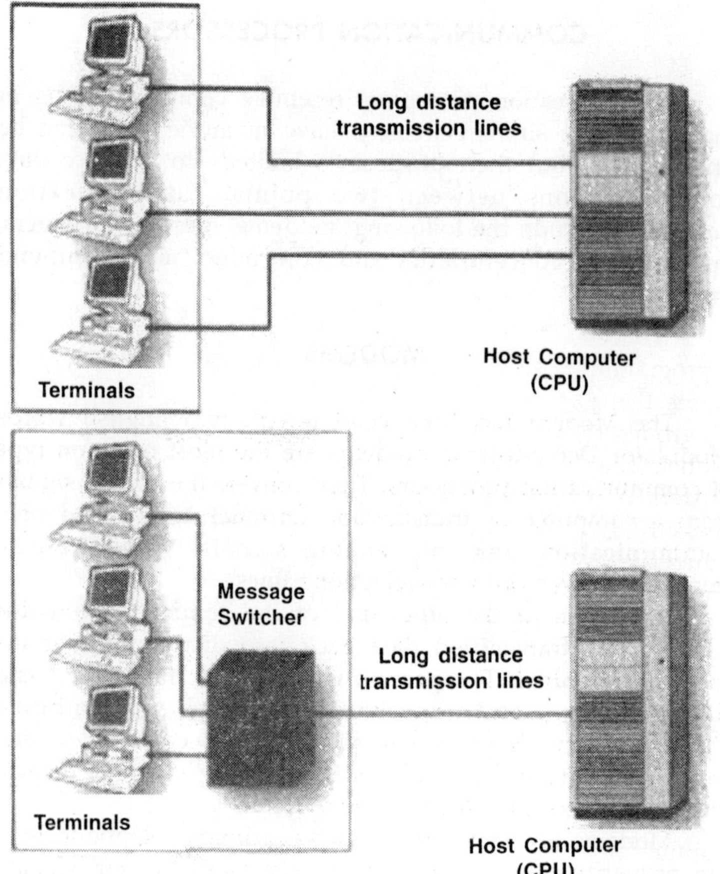

COMMUNICATION WITH AND WITHOUT MESSAGE SWITCHERS

The advantage of message switchers is that it reduces long distance transmission costs, since only a single line is needed. Although only one terminal at a time can communicate with the CPU, message switchers are efficient, with low speed terminals that are intermittently used at remotesites.

MULTIPLEXERS, CONCENTRATORS AND CONTROLLERS

Like message switchers, a multiplexer allows several terminals to use one line to communicate with a CPU. However, it allows the terminals to send their messages simultaneously. A multiplexer, in other words, collects messages from various senders, put them in order, and transmits them along a broadband channel at very high speeds to the receiver.

A concentrator is essentially a smart multiplexer—it can be programmed, has more processing capability, and is more flexible than a multiplexer. Controllers or cluster controllers, link groups of terminals or other devices to a communication channel. The controller polls the status of each terminal and transfers data from a terminal to the host computer when necessary. Multiplexers, concentrators and controllers are frequently used at terminal sites having heavy input and output requirements.

COMPONENTS OF COMMUNICATION

Front-end Processors

A front-end processor is located at the site of the CPU or the host computer and its purpose is to relieve the central computer of some of the communication tasks, leaving the larger computer free for processing applications programs.

Communication processing and data processing equipment are nearly alike. Indeed, front-end processors are computers—they have some identical circuitry and perform many of the operations that data processing equipment performs. The only difference between the two kinds of equipments is in their purpose.

COMMUNICATION NEEDS

The Communication needs several components as follows:

1. A computer to receive, process and send information called the host computers. A host computer is usually a mainframe that sends and receives data over a network. It performs a number of other important functions, such as checking the data for accuracy, sending error messages to the user if an error is found during transmission, and coordinating and controlling all data transmissions over the network.
2. Devices to send and receive information.
3. Telecommunication channels that link geographically separated devices using media such as telephone lines and cables.
4. Various types of computer hardware.
5. Various types of computer software.

COMMUNICATION MEDIA

Channels also known as communication lines or links are the means by which data are transmitted between the sending and receiving devices in a network. A channel makes use of a variety of media. These include twisted-pair wire, coaxial cables and fiber optic cables, all of which physically link the devices in a network. Also included are microwave systems, communication satellite systems and cellular radio, all of which use microwave and other radio waves to transmit and receive data. Twisted-pair Wire.

This is the oldest and still most common transmission line and consists of copper wires twisted into pairs. These lines are used in established communication networks throughout the world for both voice and data transmission.

COAXIAL CABLE

Coaxial cables consist of a sturdy copper or aluminum wire wrapped with spacers to insulate and protect it. The insulation minimizes the interference and distortion of the signals the cable carries.

Groups of coaxial cables may be bundled together in a big cable for ease of installation. These high quality lines can be placed underground and laid on the floors of lakes and oceans. They allow high-speed data transmission.

FIBER OPTIC CABLE

Fiber optics use cables consisting of one or more hair—thin filaments of glass fiber—wrapped in a protective jacket. They can conduct light pulses generated by lasers at transmission rates as high as 2 billion bits per second. This is about ten times greater than coaxial cables and 200 times better than twisted-pair wires. Fiber optic cables provide and weight reduction as well as increased speed and greater carrying capacity. A half-inch diameter fiber optic cable can carry up to 50,000 channels, compared to about 5,500 channels for a standard coaxial cable.

Fiber optic cables are not affected by and do not generate electromagnetic radiation; therefore, multiple fibers can be placed in the same cable. Fiber optic cables have a minimal need for repeaters for signal retransmissions, unlike electrical wiremedia. Fiber optics also has a much lower data error rate than other media.

3

Database Management Systems (DBMS)

Information is the backbone to any organization. It is the most critical resource of the organization. It is the indispensable link that ties together all the components of an organization for better operation and co-ordination and for survival in today's brutally competitive environment. To succeed in this environment one must manage the future. Managing the future means managing information. In this century of information explosion, where people are bombarded with data, getting the right information, in the right amount, at the right time is not an easy job. So, only those organizations that have succeeded in managing information will survive.

Data is the basis for information. When data is processed it becomes information. The data can be numerical, alphabetical or alphanumeric or any symbol.

For example, the list of students doing a particular course can be a set of data.

DATA TO INFORMATION

Data is the raw material from which information is derived as the end product. Data represents a set of characters that have no meaning on their own, i.e. it consists of just symbols. On processing, meaning is attached to data, which transforms into information.

RECORD

When interrelated data is presented in a uniform format it becomes a record. Each individual item of data stored in a record is known as a field. Each record may contain one or more than one field. For example, the name of students is a field.

RECORD LENGTH

A record may be of fixed length or variable length. A fixed-length record has a specific number of characters. For instance, if the record length is set at 30 characters and only 25 characters are used then 5 empty (unused) spaces are stored with the data.

A variable-length record is the one in which places are allotted only to data. For instance, if only 25 characters are used in a 30 character field then the storage space utilized will be only 25 characters. This method saves storage space.

WHAT IS A DATABASE?

Database means a collection of data designed to be used by different people. It is a collection of inter-related data stored together with controlled redundancy to serve one or more applications in an optimal fashion.

DATABASE MANAGEMENT SYSTEM

Database Management System (DBMS) is a collection of databases and a set of programs that are used to manipulate the data. The program or software may be used to store, delete, modify and retrieve data that is stored in a database.

DBMS acts as an interface between the users.

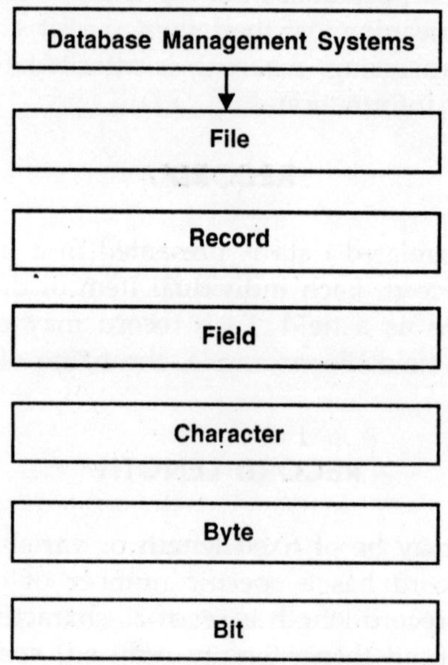

Data Hierarchy

- From this hierarchy it is clear that a database is made up of files.
- Files are composed of records. Each record consists of fields or data items.
- Each field is composed of characters, which are made up of bytes.
- And lastly, bytes decompose into bits.

DBMS permits users to search and query database contents in order to extract solution to unplanned and non-recurring problems. The users can use this package to assemble the needed data items from a common database and get solutions to their queries. It is very flexible and easy to use package.

FEATURES OF DBMS

An organization uses an integrated database to store its operational data. A database system provides the organization with centralized control of its data.

ADVANTAGES/NEED AND PURPOSES OF DBMS

The advantages of having data in a database is summarized below:

1. Redundancy can be Reduced

In non-database system, each application or department has its own private files resulting in a considerable amount of redundancy of the stored data. Thus, storage space is wasted. By having a centralized database, most of this can be avoided.

2. Inconsistency can be Avoided

This is really a corollary to the above point. When the same data is duplicated and changes are made at one site, which is not propagated, to the other site, it gives rise to inconsistency. So, if redundancy is removed, the chances of having inconsistent data is also removed.

3. Data can be Shared

The existing applications can share the data in a database.

4. Standards can be Enforced

With the central control of the database, the database administrator can enforce standards.

5. Security Restrictions can be Applied

With complete authority over the operational data, the database administrator can ensure that the only means of access to the database is through proper channels. He can define authorization checks to be carried out whenever access to sensitive data is attempted.

6. Integrity can be Maintained

Integrity means that the data in the database is accurate. Centralized control of the data helps in permitting the administrator to define integrity constraints to the data in the database.

CHARACTERISTICS OF DATA IN A DATABASE

The data in a database should have the following features:

Shared—Data in a database are shared among different users and applications.

Persistence—Data in a database exist permanently in the sense, the data can live beyond the scope of the process that created it.

Validity/Integrity/Correctness—Data should be correct with respect to the real world entity that they represent.

Security—Data should protect from unauthorized access.

Consistency—Whenever more than one data element in a database represents related real-world values, the values should be consistent with respect to the relationship.

Non-redundancy—No two data items in a database should represent the same real-world entity.

Independence—The three levels in the schema (internal, conceptual and external) should be independent of each other so that the changes in the schema at one level should not affect the other levels.

Some of the Services Provided by a DBMS are giving Below:

Database Models

A database model is an organizing principle that specifies particular mechanisms for data storage and retrieval. The model explains, in terms of services available to an interfacing application, how to access a data element when other related data elements are known.

Some of the important data models are :

- Hierarchical
- Network
- Relational
- Object-oriented

The systematic development of databases started with the hierarchical and network models, which were popular in the 1960s and 1970s.

CREATING A FILE IN FOXPRO

Let us have a general idea of features PC database system package with special reference to the most commonly used package-DBASE III PLUS or FOXBASE+ or Foxpro.

To create a database, we need to type command CREATE and press the RETURN key then it will ask us to.

Enter the name of the new file : **HARISH** (any name).

After giving the name HARISH to the file, it will ask the information about the fields in each record. For each field, it needs to know the name, type, width and number of decimal places. The structure of SRIM database looks like:

Sl. No.	*Field Name*	*Type*	*Width*	*Dec.*
1.	Author	Char	100	
2.	Title	Char	150	
3.	ACCN. No.	Numeric	15	
4.	Call No.	Alphaniumeric	20	

After entering all field names, just save this file. Every database package allows users to carry out these file-creation activities and the other operations described follow.

ENTERING DATABASE RECORDS

Once file specifications have been set, just type the command APPEND for entering the new database file.

It will bring us a form to fill out on the screen

Record No.	1
AUTHOR	RAMAN, S.
TITLE	Physics
ACCN. NO.	1
CALL NO.	C

SORTING

Generally, it is easier to read data if they are arranged in some pre-designed order. Sorting records means to arrange them in order. The sort can be numerical or alphabetical and the data can be arranged in ascending or descending order.

The field used in the sorting process is the key fields. Most database packages allow sorting by more than one key field. This would be used, for instance, while sorting names. The first key field in the sort is called the primary key while subsequent fields are the secondary key fields.

DELETING

Removing records from a file is called deleting. It is wise for the user to keep a backup copy of the file to have, in case of accidental deletion. Individual fields within a record can also be deleted. After the data are deleted, those data items are no longer available.

UPDATING

Updating is the process of changing the content of a record or records in a database file. This updating might be adding, deleting or changing the contents of a record. By accessing records and changing the field contents, the computer user can keep all the records current.

SEARCHING

Searching a file means to look through a file and to locate data. Searching for data may also be called finding or retrieving by some systems. One file at a time is searched with a file management system, but multiple files can be searched in DBMS. A database management package derives much of its power form the ease with which it can sort records and search for answers to a wide range of questions. Search questions are posed in different ways depending on the type of user interface that's built into the package. Some command-driven packages require users to supply search instructions in cryptic codes. Some menu driven packages permit users to select words and options appearing in successive menus, until they have built a search command, the program understands.

If a user is uncertain as to exactly what data he or she is looking for, an entire file can be searched, one record at a time. Listing each record in the file permits the use to visually search sometimes called "browsing" the file until the right one is located. More often, however, the user knows what data are required. With most data managers, the user can enter the search parameters to locate the specific records containing those data. Those records will be found and displayed.

STRUCTURES OF DATABASE MANAGEMENT PACKAGES

The structures of Database Management Packages are used to organize the data elements in three basic ways:

- Hierarchical database structure.
- Network database structure.
- Relational database structure.

The **Hierarchical database** structure resembles an upside-down tree with the root at the top and the branching formed below or resembles an organization chart of a corporation. The president has many vice-presidents, who have many subordinates. There's a superior-subordinate relationship in this structure. One might view structure as an upside-down family tree.

At the top level of data is the parent or root level. Data found under the root level are at the child or subordinate level. Each parent can have numerous children but each child can have only one parent. Each child level may also be broken down into further levels with becoming the parent for the next level.

The Network database structure is similar to the hierarchical structure, it is more complex but also more flexible in accessing data items. Similar to the hierarchical structure, it is more complex, but also more flexible in accessing data items. Similar to a hierarchical structure, each parent can have more than one parent. This structure permits the connection of the nodes in a multidirectional manner. Thus, each node may have several owners and may, in turn, own any number of other data units. The network database structure is a more versatile and flexible data access structure than the hierarchical type because the route of data is not necessarily downward. It can be from any direction.

RELATIONAL DATABASE MANAGEMENT SYSTEMS (RDBMS)

Short for relational database management system and pronounced as separate letters, a type of *database management system (DBMS)* that *stores data* in the form of *related tables*. Relational databases are powerful because they require few assumptions about how data is related or how it will be extracted from the database. As a result, the same database can be viewed in many different ways. An important feature of relational systems is that a single database can be spread across several tables. This differs from flat-file databases, in which each database is self-contained in a single table.

At a minimum, these systems presented the data to the user as relations (a presentation in tabular form, i.e. as a collection of tables with each table consisting of a set of rows and columns, can satisfy this property) provided relational operators to manipulate the data in tabular form.

Almost all full-scale database systems are RDBMS's. Small database systems, however, use other designs that provide less flexibility in posing queries. The Relational model is the current favorite while the object-oriented model slowly emerging and point the way to the future. The reason why the relational model is the most popular is because of its immense user base, its power to organize data, its performance as a data management tool and its many popular-commercial implementations (DB2, Oracle, Sybase, MS-SQL Server, MS-Access, etc. to name a few).

When relational model came into the scene its superiority over the existing models (hierarchical and network) was very striking. The newer models (object-oriented and deductive) do offer some advantages over the relational model. The different terms used in the relational database model are being discussed here.

a. Entities

An entity is simply a person, place, event or thing for which we intend to collect data. For example, in a university environment, entities of interest might be pilots, aircraft, routes, suppliers and any number of additional items for which data must be gathered.

b. Attributes

Each entity has certain characteristics known as attributes. For instance, the student entity might include the following attributes : Student number, major and so on. Similarly, the airline might define these attributes for its aircraft entity: aircraft number, date of last maintenance, total hours flown, hours flown since last maintenance and so on.

c. Relation

The relation is the only data structure used in the relational data model to represent both entities and the relationships between them. A relation may be visualized as a name table shows the two relations EMPLOYEE and DESIGNATION using a tabular structure. Each column of the table corresponds to an attribute of the relation and is named.

Emp-code	*Name*	*Designation*
3727	Moni Sankar	Programmer
3728	Kumar	DBA
3729	Kasi Durai	Manager
3730	Vinod	DBA
3731	Ramesh	Programmer
3721	Alisha	System Analyst

Design-code	*Designation*
321	Programmer
322	System Analyst
323	DBA
324	Manager
325	Computer Operator

d. Tuple

Row of a relation is referred to as tuple. A tuple having a set of n numbers of attribute is termed as n-tuple.

e. Domain

The values for an attribute or a column are drawn from a set of values known as a domain. The domain of an attribute contains the set of values that.

Almost all DBMSs employ SQL as their query language. Alternative query languages have been proposed and implemented, but very few have become commercial products. Access in MS OFFICE has been designed as a Relational Database Management System.

4

Library Automation

The industrial revolution, which started in Britain, brought structural changes in our society. One of the important changes was the movement of the labor force from the agricultural sector to the industrial sector. In this society, information has become the predominant element than mere industry. Thus, the post-industrial society is known as 'Information Society'. Further, the way of decision-making has considerably changed. The important feature is the use of modern technologies effectively and efficiently for various purposes. The explosion of computer and communication technologies, which are jointly termed as 'communications' or 'information technology' affected almost all aspects of human life, including library.

The purpose of starting with these two definitions is certainly to remind that the prime objective and functions of a library are not going to change by computerization, the only thing changing is the tools and techniques to achieve the defined aims and objectives with ease and accuracy.

DEFINITION OF AUTOMATION

Modernization of library housekeeping operations mainly by computerization is known as 'Library Automation'. The term 'Library Automation' in the past was used to refer to the mechanization of the traditional library operations like acquisition, serial control, cataloguing and circulation control. Today it is used to refer computerization of not only traditional library activities but also such related activities as information organization, information storage, retrieval, use, etc.

Although computers play very important role in the automation of libraries, application of telecommunication and reprography technology is also equally important.

International Encyclopedia of Information Technology and library science defines automation as 'the technology concerned with the design and development of process and system that minimize the necessity of human invention in their operation'.

UNDERSTANDING LIBRARY AUTOMATION

- Library Automation is use of machines in a Library for various activities.
- Collection: Compact Shelving, Electronic Mapping, Conveyor Belt System, Book Lift.
- Security: Close Circuit Camera Device, Electronic Security Gate.
- Users: Photocopier, Internet, Smart Card Library Ticket, Barcode Library Card.
- Library Procedures: Computer Systems, CD Station Systems, LAN.
- Environment: Power Backup, Air Conditioning, Facilities.
- E-Resources: BookEye Machine for Digitisation, Microfilm Reader and Printer, Online E-References and DBs Access.
- Multimedia Corner: Television, Audio System, Digital Audio and Video System.

THE NEED FOR AUTOMATION

The computer was invented because it was needed and it will remain, as it is needed. Its use in the library is the need of the day and its application will certainly increase the use and utility of libraries.

The need for library automation can be explained under following two headings:

- Productivity
- Accessibility

PRODUCTIVITY

Automation saves the effort, time and resources involved in the manual operation of libraries. In an automated system the information can be altered and updated without the repletion involved in the manual system.

ACCESSIBILITY

- To facilitate wider and deeper access to information.
- To increase the retrievability of the resources.
- To achieve a new level of library management.
- To improve the existing services and to introduce new services.
- To improve control over collection.
- To have an efficient control over the entire operation.
- To avoid the duplication of work.
- To facilitate sharing of the resources among various libraries.

Some of the factors that forced the libraries to go for automating the activities are:

- Information Explosion.
- Space Saving.
- Time Saving.
- Availability of information in electronic form.
- Cost effectiveness.

- Data manipulation.
- Exploitation of computer readable databases.

Thus, the application of information technology and computers can exploit the computer-based database services and Internet resources.

UNDERSTANDING MEANING OF MONITORING

- Monitoring is a review and evaluation of work Plan regularly to determine the use of standards, guides and policies.
- Monitoring is an integral part of every project from start to finish.

LIBRARY AUTOMATION MONITORING INVOLVES

- Data Input Team Work.
- Coordination of Team Members.
- Regular Data Backups.
- Re-Arrangement of Resources on Shelves.
- Use of Standard Authority (Subject Authority, Country Collection, Curriculum Areas).
- Hardware and LAN functions.
- Controlling Capital Fund.
- Users Interactions at Circulation Desk.
- Use of OPAC by Users.
- Providing Information Services to the Users.
- Use of Electronic Security Devices.
- Users Feedback on Library Automation Activities.

FACTORS AFFECTING IMPLEMENTATION OF LIBRARY AUTOMATION

Factors affecting implementation have to be properly addressed and understand for smooth functioning of the Library Automation system, these are as follows.

- Unwillingness to Change

- Low prestige given to Library and Information Work
- Lack of Management Support on Library Automation
- Understanding of Library and Information in Productivity and Quality of work within Organisation
- Lack of Leadership
- Lack of Trained Library Staff
- Fear of New Technology
- Poor Understanding of Results from New Technologies
- Limited Resources for Capital Investment
- Inability to pay running cost (e.g. software and hardware maintenance, Internet, E-Subscriptions).

LIBRARY AUTOMATION SOFTWARE ISSUES

The fundamental unit of requirement for automation is the infrastructure. The infrastructure mainly consists of the 'Computers'. The computers are the essential components of the automation. Computers that electronic device on which the automation is depended. It is that super product of electronics that is capable of performing the functions as desired by the user with maximum accuracy and quickness.

WHY AUTOMATE LIBRARY?

Library management systems are now established as an essential tool in the support of effective customer service, stock management and, in general, management of the services offered by libraries and other agencies engaged in the provision of access to collections of documents. The focus of such systems is on maintenance, development and control of the documents in the collection. Systems support selection, ordering, acquisitions, labeling, and cataloguing and circulation control of library stock. In many functions the system acts primarily as an information source on the state of the stock, and hence must hold records, which describe the stock and its whereabouts. This information makes it possible to answer questions such as "What is in stock?" or "What is on loan to whom?" Occasionally, the system may actually control the stock—for example, by using a trapping store, which triggers a light of a 'buzz' when a reserved book is returned to the circulation desk. The more current the information is, the more effective is the control of the operation. Most systems embrace the majority of the library collection. Serials, however, because of their ongoing nature, pose special problems, especially in the area of acquisitions and subscription control.

Early systems development was piecemeal, with some libraries developing cataloguing systems first, and others focusing instead on, say, circulation control systems. Current systems are integrated systems, based on relational database architecture. In such systems the files are interlinked so that deletions, additions and other changes in one file automatically activate appropriate changes in related files.

The question "Why Automate Library?" can be answered in following 3 steps:

1. Library House-keeping Operation.
2. Extension Services of above.
3. Library software performance in the context on net?

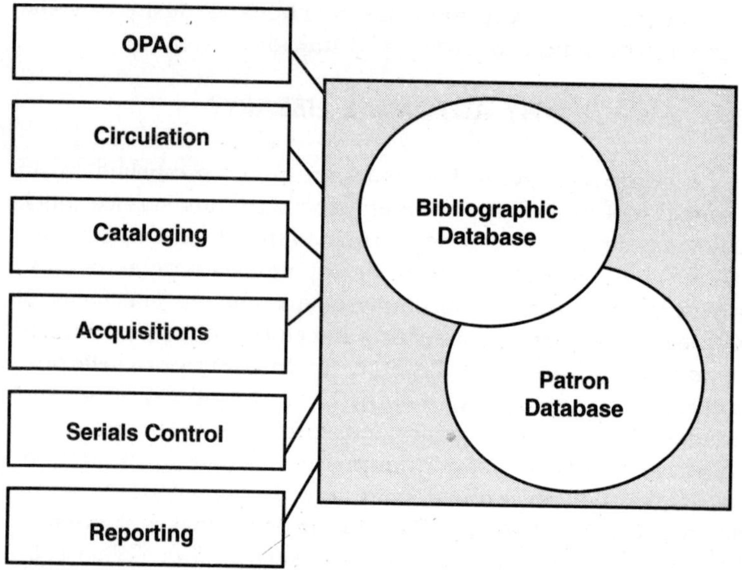

LIBRARY HOUSE KEEPING OPERATION

Typical library automation helps in acquisition system as follows:

- Pre-order searching to avoid duplication
- Creating purchase order.

  (i) Request for invoice, if necessary.
  (ii) Sending order letter.

- Receiving materials.

  (i) Compilation of accession list.
  (ii) Announcement of latest documents received.
  (iii) Compilation of cataloguing.

- Claims (for damaged materials) and/or cancellation notice.
- Providing information to the management on orders outstanding and sometimes on work-in-progress i.e., books received but not yet catalogued.
- Maintaining book fund accounts and printing book funds reports.

FUNCTION OF LIBRARY AUTOMATION IN SERIAL CONTROLS

- Inputting serial data.
- Ordering new serials.
- Renewals of presently subscribed serials.
- Cancellation of presently subscribed serials, if necessary.
- Accessioning of individual issues as and when the issues are received.
- Sending reminders, if necessary.
- Claiming the issue (such as, request for replacement of a defective copy).
- Selective follow-up of missing issues.
- Preparation of various lists like:

(i) List of periodicals received during a specified period.

(ii) List of holding with their status on shelf, on binding, on circulation, etc. (the lists can be by subject, by country, by origin, by title, etc.).

(iii) List of periodicals cancelled during specified period.

- Keeping track of the amount spent on serials subscriptions, serials binding, etc. (subject-wise, if necessary).
- Estimation of the budget for the next academic financial year.
- Binding control.

FUNCTION OF LIBRARY AUTOMATION IN CIRCULATION SECTION

To achieve the objectives of the circulation section, the circulation system is designed to record and manipulate the information about the borrower, document and transaction. In addition to the primary function of the circulation system, i.e. charging and discharging of documents, library automation performs following function:

1. Provision of information on the location of circulation items-either all the items or only those items on loan or elsewhere, i.e., at the bindery, on reserve, being re catalogued etc.
2. Identification of items on loan to particular borrower or class of borrowers.
3. Recording of holds or personal reserves for items on loan but desired by another borrower, often with additional provision for notifying the library staff when the item is returned and printing of book available notice to the user about the availability of document.
4. Printing recall notices for items on long-term loan, when required by other.

5. Renewal of loans.
6. Notification to the library staff of overdue items and printing of overdue notices.
7. Notification to the delinquent borrowers (i.e., those with unpaid fines/or overdue book) either at the time of an attempted loan, or at the time a borrower is leaving the institution or on request from the library.
8. Calculation and printing various type of statistics.
9. Analysis of both summary statistics and statistics for the circulation of particular items for use in acquisitions, planning of services and for other administrative purposes.
10. For handling special categories of borrowers and special types of materials.
11. For printing due date slips, automatically generating orders for lost books or additional copies and printing mailing labels for remote borrowers.

FUNCTION OF LIBRARY AUTOMATION IN CATALOGUING

Cataloguing is an important work of the library. It has rightly been said that catalogue is the key to the library. It facilitates the search of books by various approaches like author, subject, title, etc. The other functions include,

- Printing of catalogue cards in different formats like book form, card form.
- Printing in different formats like AACR2 and CCC.
- Printing of added entry cards.
- Generation of Union Catalogue.

EXTENSION SERVICES IN LIBRARY

Other functions of the library automation software include:

- Storage and retrieval of information regarding books, periodicals and other materials.

- Abstracting service.
- Indexing Service.
- SDI service.
- Preparation of Union Catalogue.
- Online Public Access Catalogue (OPAC), with search facility by author, title, publisher, subject, keyword, accession number, ISBN/ISSN, etc.
- Search browse, edit, review, delete and printing of data from database.
- Preparation of mailing list.
- Report generation in different forms, including statistical reports.
- Keeping track of stock verification.
- Exporting and importing of data.
- Bar code generation, etc.

LIBRARY AUTOMATION PERFORMANCES IN THE CONTEXT OF INTERNET

Apart from the general functions mentioned above, the library automation also functions to incorporate the recent advances in the information technology. Some of the features are as follows:

(i) Access to Internet through OPAC.
(ii) Cataloguing of Internet Website.
(iii) Cataloguing of electronic documents like word processing file, spread sheets, databases, etc.
(iv) Multimedia facility.
(v) Online ordering of documents through Internet.
(vi) Booking of resources for specific time/period.
(vii) Library map indication the current position of the document in the library.
(viii) Facility for self-circulation by user.
(ix) Presence of book wizard showing the picture of the cover, review and relative information about documents.
(x) Visual information or graphic information retrieval.

Hence, Library Automation has become a necessity in

today's environment to Perform the library activities more efficiently, effectively and quickly.

WHICH LIBRARY AUTOMATION SOFTWARE TO USE?

Software is the other essential component of the computer system. It is the main component that makes the computer to manipulate data. Software is a set of programs that determine the processing of the computer. Without software the computer is just a machine. Software is the main interface between the machine and man. It is responsible for the processing whether numerical or logical. Different software packages are present for different applications.

DEFINITION OF SOFTWARE

Software is a set of programs and a program is a set of commands. In other words, software is a computer program for using computers and other such hardware to their optimum capabilities. As computers do only what they are told to do and therefore, the instructions given to computer should be unambiguous. Writing step-by-step instructions without any ambiguity to solve a particular problem is called 'Programming'.

A Software package can have one or more computer programs to solve a specific problem. A programming language provides a special type of grammar and syntax to the programmer to enable him/her to give instructions in a simple and understandable way. Writing programs and developing software packages involves special training, hard work, time and money. For developing in-house software to solve complex problems these requirements become severe and unmanageable. Due to these limitations, the practicing librarians or information scientists are going for commercial software packages instead of in-house developed.

TYPES OF SOFTWARE

We write programs or develop software packages for computer to enable the computer to do some specific or general jobs depending on the needs of the users. On the basis of the purpose of the software they may be classified into 3 broad categories. They are:

APPLICATION SOFTWARE

These are programs employed by the user to perform some specific functions. For example, application software can be a program used for inventory control in business or a program used by the library professionals for the library house keeping activities. (The commercial software's like LIBSYS, Sanjay, Maitrayee, etc.)

SYSTEMS SOFTWARE

Systems software consists of all the programs, languages, and documentation supplied by the manufacturer with the computer. These programs allow the user to communicate with the computer and write or develop his/her own programs. This software makes the machine easier to use and makes very efficient use of the resources of the hardware. System software are programs held permanently on a machine, which will relieve the programmer from some mundane tasks and will improve resource utilization.

Examples: WINDOWS, UNIX, etc.

UTILITY SOFTWARE

This may be considered as application software or systems software, which is used quite often in the development of a program. For example, a program for the evaluation of logarithm or square root of a number may be required in developing some applications software. The user depending upon his area writes application software and Utility software.

CATEGORIES OF LIBRARY SOFTWARE

Computerization of library and information services, involves non-numeric data processing, text retrieval, manipulation of strings of characters, and information can be used for these purposes and for specific needs, special purpose software are also available in the market. The various categories of such software and their features are: Basic software for data entry, validation, sorting, merging of files, and editing of data.

Word processing software to manipulate text-storage, recall, use and modify; alignment of margins, addition and deletion of string of characters, manipulate paragraphs, etc.

Text-retrieval packages for storage and retrieval of non-numeric record (tabular and even graphics). These are self-contained software, require minimum involvement of computer specialists, records are independent of variable length for natural language, text, have access to data by context, inverted file access, user interfaces which makes them simple and easy to use. Software Associated with searching online retrieval system and CD-ROM databases. Major online systems have their own software usually written in command language, provide access to external databases. Private or personal file facility and permit editing of search files on micros.

LIBRARY HOUSE KEEPING SOFTWARE

These have provision for acquisition, cataloguing, circulation control, serial control and statistical report generation. Library automation software or computer-based information storage and retrieval systems cover two major functional areas, namely;

1. Control and management of library resources
2. Access to documents and information

These two areas deal with library house-keeping systems and text retrieval systems respectively. Gradually, the distinction between them in vanishing, in latest software packages there is provision for both library house-keeping operations as well as public access for information retrieval.

In addition, there are software packages for re-organizing and presenting information in desired format, producing publications, control and to manipulate statistical and financial data. Library automation software packages can also be grouped in 4 categories.

- ✓ Word Processing
- ✓ Library House-keeping Operations
- ✓ Management Communications and support
- ✓ Text retrieval

Each of these categories of software may be either In-house developed software that is owned and operated by the library, or shared with other libraries through a consortium arrangement through a bibliographic information network.

STRATEGY FOR SOFTWARE SELECTION AND EVALUATION

When considering a new computer system a strategy for evaluation and selection and for the management of the project is essential. Such a strategy can be exploited both to assist in choosing an appropriate software package, and to design the system that will be created with the software package. Very often the time involved in the selection and implementation of a computer system is seriously underestimated leading to late implementation, unfulfilled expectations and other associated hazards.

The strategy, which is proposed below, assumes that the systems project evolves form application to software and hardware. In other words, the requirements of the application are identified, prior to the introduction of constraints that may be posed by hardware and software. Sometimes hardware has already been purchased, or it is desirable to adhere to externally imposed hardware and software standards. A model for strategy for the selection and evaluation of library software packages is proposed on next page.

DIFFERENT LIBRARY AUTOMATION MANAGEMENT SOFTWARE

Freeware

Freeware includes any software for which the author and/or Publisher seek no remuneration whatsoever from the user for the full software package. (I.e., freeware must be able to perform some useful function in and of itself, and not only in conjunction with a "scaled-up" version of the submitted software). Third-party "add on" and "plug ins" to commercial products such as Filmmaker or PhotoShop may still be considered freeware, as long as there is no charge for the use of the entire add-on or plug-in. Freeware may be either copyrighted or public domain. Most "open source" titles will be considered freeware, though products don't by any means have to be open-source to be freeware (i.e., binaries without source distribution are freeware as long as they meet the other criteria). Software that is free for private use but fee-based for commercial use may also be considered freeware. Several freewares are available for library automation.

Ex: Koha, Open Book, CDS/ISIS, etc.,

CDS/ISIS

CDS/ISIS stands for Computerised Documentation System, Integrated Set of Information System. CDS/ISIS mini micro version 3.07 is a UNESCO released licensed software distributed in India through NISSAT. Manual provided with the version 3.0 holds good for version 3.07 also the following account is an extract from the CDS/ISIS manual for version 3.07.

CDS/ISIS has brought out.

WINISIS, JAVA ISIS for Windows platforms today.

One can create, build and manage an unlimited number of structured non-numerical data bases. One may think of the data bases as files. In all these files, each unit of information is made up of elementary data elements which one may define and manipulate in various ways:

- Define data bases and Enter new records
- Modify, correct and delete records
- Automatically build and maintain fast access files in each data base
- Retrieve records
- Sort the records and Display the records
- Print catalogues and/or indexes

CDS/ISIS Package contains two programs namely

- ❖ User Program
- ❖ System Programs

USER PROGRAMS (MENUS)

E - ISISENT = Data entry and record editing
S - ISISRET = Information and retrieval
P - ISISPRT = Printed outputs
I - ISISINV = Inverted file maintenance

SYSTEM PROGRAMS (MENUS)

D - ISISDEF Defining new data bases and modifying existing data base definitions
U - ISISUTL Utility functions
M - ISISXCH Interchanging data with other systems (import and export data)
A - ISISPAS Programming facilities (not covered)

MENUS

The operations to be performed are chosen from menus. A menu is a list of functions from which one can make his/her choice by typing a single letter.

PROMPTS

Once an option is selected, one should choose another option to complete the request. A 'prompt' will be blinking and the user must reply by typing a file name which will be the database name.

Example : Data Base name: Balu

Here the chosen name should be typed without any spelling error. Any spelling is accepted if it is a new database. To call an already existing database the exact spelling should be typed otherwise, the system replies 'Database does not exist'. It will give chances till you spell out the exact characters of the database name.

WORKSHEETS

Normally we use a printed sheet to fill in data. Here, a worksheet is a particular screen layout used to enter data. Similar to a pre-printed form, a worksheet contains a number of fields each of which consist of the field name and an empty line where the corresponding data can be keyed (typed) in. In some cases the same data may be recurring in many of the records and has to be entered in more than one record. In such cases you can fix such data permanently in the worksheet. Such a fixed data is called a "default value".

The maximum number of fields in a worksheet page is 19 and the maximum number of pages in a worksheet is 20.

There are two types of worksheets

System worksheets: Designed by CDS/ISIS instead of a prompt to ask for additional information.

Data entry worksheets: Used to create or modify a data base record. Because data entry worksheet must be tailored for different databases. CDS/ISIS provide you with a worksheet editor to set-up these worksheets according to the requirements.

THE CDS/ISIS DATABASE

The term "AUTHOR" is known as field.

RANGANATHAN, S.R. is a data element for the Author field.

Each unit of information which is stored in the data base consists of discrete data elements, each describing a particular characteristic. Data elements are stored in fields, each of which is assigned a numeric tag. The collection of fields is called a record.

CDS/ISIS is designed to handle fields of varying length.

A field may be optional. It may contain a single data element, or two or more elements of varying length. In the latter case the field is said to contain subfields, each of which is identified by a 2-character "subfield delimiter".

^a	^b	^c
Some	fields may be	repeatable

MASTER FILE

The Master file contains all the records of a given database. Individual records are identified by a unique number, automatically assigned by CDS/ISIS when they are created called the Master File Number or MFN.

To provide fast access to each master file record, CDS/ISIS associates a special file to the Master file, called the Cross reference File. It is a pointer giving the location of each record in the Master file.

INVERTED FILE

The inverted file is essentially an index to the contents of the Master file.

The searchable elements for a given data base are defined by the user in a Field Select Table (FST). It contains the fields to be inverted (indexed) and the indexing technique to be used for each field.

Please note that the elements will be truncated after 30 characters. In other words, the index known as terms dictionary displays it in two columns per page and each column cannot exceed 30 characters.

DEFINITION OF DATA STRUCTURE

When creating a database you must define the data structure. In CDS/ISIS the data strueture definition includes the creation of a FDT, a worksheet, a FST and a display format. The other supporting files will be developed by the system itself.

ISISDEF

Avoid editing when you are defining your FDT, worksheet and FST for your database as this may cause your database to be rejected in the ISISENT program. If you have made any errors during the first definition phase then edit the FDT, worksheet and FST after your data base has been accepted in the ISISNT program.

FIELD DEFINITION TABLE (FDT)

The maximum number of fields in a record which can be defined is 200.

Tag : A numeric value, identifying field (range 1-32767).

Name : A descriptive name not more than 30 characters long.

Length : The maximum number of characters which can be stored in a field (range 1-1650). Default value is 100 characters. Note that if you need more than 1650 characters you must define the field as repeatable.

Type : Indicating the possible restrictions of the data characters.

X = alphanumeric (default).
A = alphabetic,
N = numeric,
P = pattern.

Repeatable: If a field may occur more than once in a record this is indicated with a R. A repeatable field can contain subfields.

Subfields: Indicating the name and the order of the number of subfields. No subfield delimiter code (^) is entered. Here the subfields can be denoted by characters only.

Pattern: A character-by-character description of the content of the field. A = alphabetic, X = alphanumeric, 9 = numeric, other = any indicated character. Note that 'A' and 'X' must be entered in uppercase, that the maximum length of a pattern is 20 characters, that a pattern field can not be repeatable, and that it can not contain subfields.

WORKSHEET CREATION

The worksheet is the format or frame which one can use later for data entry in the ISISENT programs, when creating a worksheet use the worksheet editor which will prompt you to give the values mentioned below for each field.

Field tag : Give the tag number defined in the FDT or a ? to display the tag and name of each field or a T indicate title field.

Name Position: Give the line and column (L/C) position to indicate where the name of a specific field is to be placed on the screen. There are 21 lines and 80 columns on the screen. A negative number between -21 and -1 produces a ruler at the screen.

Field value: Give the line and column (L/C) position to indicate where you want the data entry part to begin at the screen. There exist same options as mentioned under Name position.

Field attribute: The system gives you a choice of 6 attributes. Note that these can be modified in the ISISUTL service.

Field length: This must be given in number of characters or in lines, e.g. 250 (number of characters defined in your FDT) or L4 (gives 4 lines counted from the beginning of the data entry).

For repeatable and non-repeatable fields you can define scrolling line e.g. instead of 250 characters one can write S3 which gives you a scrolling field with a 3 line window. Whenever you reach the end of line 3 in data entry a new line will appear "scrolling". When defining the length as scrolling you can exceed the maximum field length given in the FDT.

Help message: Maximum 2 lines of text which will be displayed by pressing <F1> in data entry (ISISENT).

Define value: One can give any value which will be displayed whenever one calls the data entry worksheet. Note that default values can also be given in the ISISENT service.

If one uses line 21 when you define your worksheet it may stop one from going to the next page and thereby stopping the worksheet creation. Note that you can define as many worksheets as one may need for each data base.

FIELD SELECT TABLE (FST)

The Field Select Table is used for creating the Inverted File. The inverted file is an index of terms along with their occurrence in the fields. The first FST you create indicates primarily the fields you want to index for later searching in the ISAISRET service.

A line editor enables to create the FST. For each field to be indexed the following values must be given as indicated follow:

FIELD IDENTIFIER (ID)

For all the fields that should be searchable they should be provided with a tag number (1..2..3.. or 10..20..30..). The latter is preferable.

INDEXING TECHNIQUE (IT)

You can Choose Among Five Indexing Techniques:

0 = builds an element from each line. The whole field is indexed, but as lines.

1 = builds an element from each subfield and/or line exit-acted by the format. One can specify MPL in Data Exit-action Format (or leave it out as MPL is Default).

2 = builds and element from each or phrase enclosed in triangular brackets <>. One can specify MPL in Data Extraction Format (or leave it out as MPL is default).

3 = same as two, but term or phrase enclosed in slashes//.

4 = builds an element from each "word" in the text, Note if the field you are indexing contains subfield delimiters you must specify MHL.

The keyword index in ISISRET service can be created by all techniques. Make that the elements will be truncated after 30 characters.

DATA EXTRACTION FORMAT

Hence, the format of the data to be extracted from a record has to be specified. Give a "Mode indicator" followed by the Tag prefixed by a 'V'(v10).

DEFINITION OF DISPLAY FORMAT

ISISDEF

The display format can be used for screen as well as paper display. The maximum number of characters in a single display format is 4000. Before creating a display format you must make a model of how wish your data to be displayed on the screen and/or on paper.

The display format allows you to define precise formatting requirements for data base records. You can select the specific data elements in the order you want and insert constant text of your choice, as well as specify vertical and horizontal spacing requirements.

Note that you can define as many display formats as you need for each data base.

FIELD SELECT PARAMETER

The General Format for a Field Select Parameter is as Given Overleaf

Vtt^X

where

V	:	Field code
tt	:	two digit number indicating the field tag
^X	:	subfield delimiter code indicating that only the contents of the subfield is to be displayed

The Format is Illustrated through the Following Example:

Field name	input two subfields (tag = 4)
City, Country	^A Jakarta^B Indonesia
Format	Output
V4	Jakarta, Indonesia
V4^B	Indonesia

The field select parameter can be used in connection with all the display format parameters described in the following.

Literals

One may insert constants called literals in the output to improve legibility. A literal consist of string of characters enclosed between delimiters.

- Unconditional literals
- Conditional literals
- Repeatable literals

UNCONDITIONAL LITERALS

Unconditional literals are always included in the output regardless of the presence or absence of the field in a record. Unconditional literals are enclosed is single quote marks (').

Note that the length of an unconditional literal may not exceed the line width.

Example

(Display format) MFN(4), '-', MDL, V24/'Author(s): 'V70/##

(Output)

0027 - Measurement of dry matter productions of the plant cover. Author(s). Woodwell, George M. Bourdeau, Philippe F.

0028 - Scientific Problems of the humid tropical zone deltas and their implications proceedings of the Dacca Symposium. Author(s).

CONDITIONAL LITERALS

Conditional literals are only included in the output if the associated field is present in the record. If the associated field select parameter specifies a repeatable field, the literal will only be included once, regardless of the number of occurrences of the field. Conditional literals are enclosed in double quote marks (").

Example

(Display format) MFN (4), '-'. MDL, V24/"Author9s): "V70/##

(Output)

0027 - Measurement of dry matter productions of the plant cover.
Author(s).
Woodwell, George M. Bourdeau, Philippe F.

0028 - Scientific Problems of the humid tropical zone deltas and their implications proceedings of the Dacca Symposium.

REPEATABLE LITERALS

Repeatable literals are conditional literals, which will be repeated for each occurrence of the repeatable field. The repeatable literal will not be displayed if the associated field is empty. Repeatable literals can be associated with non-repeatable fields. Repeatable literals are enclosed in vertical bars (|).

Example repeatable field (V70) :
(Display format) MFN, '-', MDL, V24, |(|V70|)|/##
(Output)
0027 - Measurement of dry matter productions of the plant cover.
(Woodwell, George M.) (Bourdeau, Philippe F.)
028 - Scientific Problems of the humid tropical zone deltas and their implications proceedings of the Dacca Symposium.

Example non-repeatable field (V24) :
(Display format) MFN(4), '-'. MDL, |*|V24|*|,V70/##
(Output)
0027 - *Measurement of dry matter productions of the plant cover* Woodwell, George M. Bourdeau, Philippe F.
0028 - *Scientific Problems of the humid tropical zone deltas and their implications proceedings of the Dacca Symposium*.

PREFIX-LITERAL

A conditional and/or a repeatable prefix-literal is literal followed by a '+' sign (e.g. |... |+) The literal will be displayed before all but the first occurrence of the associated field.

Example

(Display format) MFN,' -',MDL.V24,|* |+V70/##
(Output)
0027 - Measurement of dry matter productions of the plant cover. Woodwell,George M. *Bourdeau, Philippe F.
0028 - Scientific Problems of the humid tropical zone deltas and their implications proceedings of the Dacca Symposium.

SUFFIX-LITERAL

A conditional and/or a repeatable post-literal is a literal preceded by a '+' sign (e.g. +|...|) The literal will be displayed after all but the last occurrence of the associated field.

(Display format) MFN, '-',MDL,V24,V70+|;|/#
(Output)
0027 - Measurement of dry matter productions of the plant cover.
Woodwell, George M. Bourdeau, Philippe F.
0028 - Scientific Problems of the humid tropical zone deltas and their implications proceedings of the Dacca Symposium.

LENGTH OF LITERALS

The maximum length of unconditional literals, conditional literal and repeatable pre-literal, is 13219 characters. The maximum length of post-literals is 50 characters. No literal may exceed the line width.

SPACING PARAMETERS

Different parameters control horizontal and vertical spacing. They are as follows:

Xn inserts 'n' spaces before formatting the next field.
Cn tabulate to line position 'n'.

Terminates and skip to new line (if the previous line is non-blank.)

- # leaves one line space
- ## leaves two lines space
- % deletes previously formatted blank line or lines (used in case a /used creates a blank line despite the absence of a previous field)

INDENTION COMMAND

The display starts at the first character position and extends up to the eighteenth character position and the overflowing data commences from the first character position of the next line.

Indention command is used to alter this default positions.

In case you want the data to be displayed from a particular position and want the continuation to start from a particular character position then this is the provision.

EXAMPLE

V10(5,8) The commencing line of the Data for V10 will be from the 5th character position and the continuation line of the data will commence from the 8th character position.

MFN COMMAND

To extract the MFN of a record, MFN or MFN (D) where (D) is the number of digits to be displayed.

MODE COMMAND

The display of data can be in three different modes as

- Proof Mode

- Heading Mode
- Data Mode

Characters used for this command are M P H D U L

M stands for Mode.
P stands for Proof mode (displays delimiters used during data entry).
H stands for Heading Mode (delimiters are ignored).
D stands for Data (delimiters are ignored and in addition a full stop is fixed at the end of each field).
U stands for UPPER case letters in display.
L stands for lower case letters in display.

Now the data structure definition is complete and data entry can be proceeded.

DATA ENTRY

ISISNET

Now data can be entered in the worksheet defined in the ISISDEF program. Note that if there is an error message "base does not exist" it may be because you have edited during the creation of the FDT and/or worksheet; or that the data base name is more than 6 characters long. The database has to be created again if this error message appears.

Before starting the data entry the default values can be defined temporarily. Note that if there are more than one worksheet the default values must be defined in each worksheet as and when they are called: Data entry rules.

Beware for using control characters as " data character"

(e.g. '^', '//', etc.).

"Blanks" are whenever a doubt arise in entering data in a field the help messaged can be displayed by pressing <F1>.

When there is a subfield the required subfield delimiter must be keyed-in front of each subfield. Do not leave 'spaces or insert punctuation marks either before or after the subfield delimiters'.

Use '%' sign to separate occurrences in repeatable fields, there must be no "blanks" around the '%' sign. Use triangular brackets' Û ' or slashed '//' to enclose words in the text which may be used as index words. A space must precedes and follow the slashes or open and closed bracket respectively if a ' natural looking ' text display or print is required. If the triangular brackets are used to delimit keywords alone no spaces shall precede and follow the bracket Note that if a slash '/' has to be displayed in the display use two slashes. The slashes will not be substituted by punctuation marks.

To move text from one field to another or to record use Cut and Paste. Mark beginning of text by pressing function key<F3>, mark end of text by pressing function key <F4>, insert text by pressing junction key <F5>.

Note that a scrolling field is longer than the space shown at the screen.

FILLING INFORMATION FOR SORTING

When producing printed catalogues one will need to sort the contents of one or more fields according to normally accepted filling rules. The filling information can be supplied at the time of data entry.

Entry	Sorted	Displayed
<The>man	Man	The Man

If a word is enclosed in triangular brackets it will be ignored while sorting, but displayed when printing.

Entry	Sorted	Displayed
<2=Two>days	Two days	2 days

If a text is indicated as equal to another within triangular brackets, the ' equal to text' will be used for sorting, but not displayed when printing

Note that fields with filling information must not be indexers with indexing technique '2' as the triangular brackets will be identified as search term delimiters by the system and the word(s) within the brackets as index terms.

There may be problems with the filling information while creating the index (dictionary list) with indexing techniques other than 4. If one wants to use filling information for sorting be needs to make two data entries in data entry worksheet. One with the filling information and one without.

EDITING

Editing: Do not call more records than you need to edit.

CDS/ISIS will go through all the records when the editing is finished in order to update the inverted file, this takes a long time.

Note that a search can be made in ISISRET and after wards edit the last set of records retrieved by using the ' R : option in the Data Bade maintenance Menu.

Delete: Records flagged for deletion can always be restored. A record is not Physically depleted until the Master file is reorganized.

INVERTED FILE GENERATION

ISISINV

Use option F whenever a database is initially created. If you are handling a very big database then create the inverted file in steps using G + S + C.

The updating of the inverted file can be done at the exit of the ISIS program. If there is a modification in the FST then the inverted file must be re-created. Adding a new field to the FST does not require re-creation of the inverted file.

Information Retrieval Process

This is based on the inverted files created in accordance with the variables defined in the FST. You can choose a terms occurring in a field variable identified in the FST. When you use a term that does not occur in any of the fields defined in the FST, then the system will say No records found. Terms sandwiched with marks specified to be indexed during data entry can also be retrieved.

The search expression can be a term or a variable field number and then the specific terms.

SEARCH EXPRESSION

RANG NATHAN, S.R.	OR
RANGANATH$	OR
?v10= 'RANG NATHAN, S.R.'	(PRESS ENTER)

COMMERCIAL SOFTWARE

Using the definition of commercial from the dictionary it indicates, "Having profit as a chief aim". This make Commercial Software to simply be software used in a commercial environment, or software developed that has "profit as a chief aim".

Many people are incorrectly using this phrase interchangeably with "Proprietary Software", and are trying to perpetuate the myth that the only way to make money in the software world is to make the software proprietary. This definition of the word "commercial" does not specify a specific way of making money, and anyone in the "Free Software", "Open Source" or similar movements know that there is more than just a single way to make money in the software world.

Phrases such as "Free Software", "Open Source Software", or "Proprietary Software" are totally independent of whether or not the software is commercial or not. Software can be licensed with the GPL or BSD License, and yet have profited as a chief aim, such as with Red Hat Software. There is also going to be proprietary software, which is given away for free (Internet Explorer and Netscape are two popular examples) where profit is not the aim of the software, but other motivations such as market control or advertising or Internet Portals.

Commercial software is software being developed by a business, which aims to make money from the use of the software. "Commercial" and "proprietary" are not the same thing! Most commercial software is proprietary, but there is commercial free software, and there is non-commercial non-free software.

Ex: LIBRARIAN, LIBSYS, SLIM++, EASYLIB, NEW GENLIB, etc ...

A SAMPLE OF REQUEST FOR PROPOSAL

- Table of Contents
- Introduction
    - o Background information on the Library
    - o General rules and conditions for submission
    - o Proposal format
- Instructions to vendors
- Training and documentation
- Functional and Technical specifications
- Database creation
- Maintenance
- Delivery and Installation scheduling and site preparation
- Performance specifications
- Acceptance tests
- Warranties
- Cost proposal

LIBRARY AUTOMATION STEPS

Planning is time-consuming, but it is usually cost-effective because time spent planning reduces the amount of time required for system implementation. Steps involved are:

Step 1: Describing existing library services and technology.

- Identifying existing services and functions provided by the library.

- Identifying existing technology being used in the library.
- Collecting and organizing basic statistical data.

Step 2: Assessing needs and setting priorities.

- Who should be involved in planning?
- Needs assessment.
- Identifying approaches to satisfy the needs.
- Setting priorities.
- Developing a preliminary budget.

Step 3: Translating needs and priorities into specifications.

- Designing specifications.
- Preparing and distributing the Request for Proposal (RFP).

Step 4: Evaluating proposals and selecting a system.

- Making the first cut.
- Seeing system demonstrations.
- Analyzing vendor responses.
- Costs.
- Obtaining responses from vendor's clients.
- Making the final cut.

Step 5: Putting your system into place.

- Contract negotiations.
- Hardware and software installation.
- Training.

Step 6: Retrospective conversion and barcoding.

AUTOMATION COSTS

- Planning and consulting costs
- Purchase of the system, hardware, and software

- Purchase of network-specific hardware, software, and cabling.
- Internet connection costs.
- Conversion of manual records into machine-readable form.
- Access, and subscriptions where appropriate, to external databases and systems.
  - Ongoing operating costs.
  - Maintenance of system hardware and software.

5

Koha

Koha is integrated library management system developed by Horowhenua Library Trust and Katipo Communications Ltd, New Zealand. It is open source software under in GNU public license it is a library and collection management system. It is designed to manage physical collections of items (books, CD's, videos, reference, etc.). It provides cataloguing,

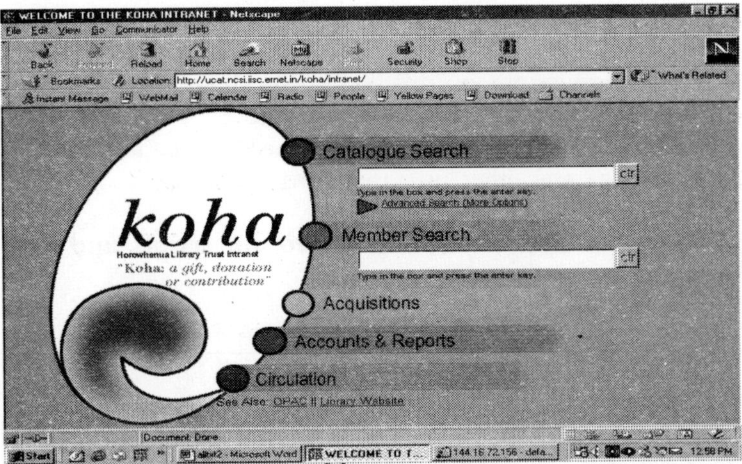

Searching, Member/patron management, an acquisitions system, and circulation (issues, returns, and reserves). Circulation is handled with a full screen curses interface or a Web-based interface. It has OPAC and cataloguing, acquisition circulation modules.

INSTALLATION ON LINUX

(1) Create a new MySQL database called for example, Koha
(2) Set-up a username and password in MySQL
(3) Use the MySQL script to create the tables

mysql –u username –p password Koha < koha.mysql here you give username password to login.

(4) Edit koha.conf

Set the database name to what you have called your database, hostname will probably stay as local host (unless you are installing the database on a different machine to the web server).

User and password should be changed to reflect the username and password you have chosen above.

(5) Copy koha.conf to /etc./

The permissions on this config file should also be strict, since they contain the database password.

At a minimum, the apache user needs to be able to read it, as well as any other user that runs circulation.

(6) Here we need to decide where our scripts and html files will be:

edit C4/Output.pm to reflect that.

Set $path as below.

$path="/usr/local/www/html/koha/opac/includes";

Next copy the C4 directory (in scripts/) to somewhere in your perl path

e.g. /usr/local/lib/site_perl/i386-linux/
Now how to set-up our OPAC

(1) Set-up a webspace for the OPAC
E.g. we can make/usr/local/www/html/opac ...
And set a virtual host in apache to use that directory
(2) In your OPAC dir make a dir called htdocs, and copy everything in opac-html/to it.
(3) Again in your OPAC dir make a dir called cgi-bin and copy all the files in scripts/that have a .pl extension to it,
E.g. copy scripts/*.pl/usr/local/www/cgi-bin/koha/
(4) Your virtual host should be set up to use these directories, e.g.,
<VirtualHost opac.your.site>
ServerAdmin webmaster@your.site
DocumentRoot /usr/local/www/opac/htdocs
ServerName opac.your.site
ErrorLog logs/opac-error_log
TransferLog logs/opac-access_log
</VirtualHost>
(5) Ok, restart apache and point your browser to OPAC.

Now we can set up the intranet/librarian interface

(1) Set-up another webspace lets call it koha for example
(2) In the dir you have just created make an htdocs dir a cgi-bin dir

Copy everything in intranet-html/to the htdocs dir
Copy all the .pl files in scripts/to the cgi-in/koha dir

(1) Make sure your virtual host is set up to use these directories
(2) Restart apache and site will start working.

PREREQUISITES

Hardware

Processor: Pentium II

RAM: 32MB
Disk size: 250MB
Computer monitor:(colour/SVGA (800*600 colour VESA compatible)
Operating system: Linux
Printer: HP LaserJet compatible

Network Interface Cards

Barcode Reader: barcode Reader should preferable interface with the keyboard connection. Barcode reader can also be supplied by soft link
UPS-500VA

Software

Apache: web server
Perl
MySQL: wwww.MySQL.com/downlode
Perl Module: Date: : manip
"http://search.cpan.org/search?dist=DateManip"
DBI (A Perl module used for the connection, retrieval and storage of data from various database application)
DBD::MySQL (or whatever database system you use)
AuthenDBI (if you want to use Database based authentication)

FEATURES (DIFFERENT MODULES SUPPORTED)

Koha Supports Following Modules

Acquisitions
Cataloguing
Membership modules
Report generation
Circulation
OPAC

Acquisition

The acquisition and ordering process has particularly benefited from computerization, as it is a relatively simple clerical process, where similar operation is applicable to all categories of library. The acquisition system in Koha is as follows:

ORDERING

While ordering a book for the library a search menu is given where before ordering one can check if similar copy is available in the library from the records. If no records are found or more number of copies are required then it can be ordered. Another search box is given where supplier ID or name can be searched, and order can be placed. If the required supplier is not available in the records then it can be added in to the records. The supplier details such as Name of the company, address such as postal and physical, phone, fax, website, current status i.e., if the company is active or inactive details can be furnished. Along with these in Koha, the person to be contacted for any details and his position e-mail, phone etc., can be furnished. Ordering information such as publishers and imprints, invoice, GST registration, discount on the article purchased can be given. While ordering for a book, bibliographic details should be given in Catalogue details which includes Title which is mandatory field, author, copyright date, format, ISBN, series, Branch (If more than one branch of the library are located at different places). The accounting details regarding quantity, book fund, suppliers list price, replacement cost, budgeted cost, budgeted GST, budgeted total, actual cost, invoice number, notes if any need to be keyed in. After providing all the above details in respective fields click on the button "Add Order". This gives the information about the order, invoice number, the title that has been ordered, author and its amount. This is known as Shopping Basket. Once the order has been received then fill in the form which is known as supplier invoice information including fields supplier invoice number, freight, number of items. The receipt information includes invoice number, the person who received and date is added in the given field. The acquisition module also contains details about the different currencies such as USA, England and Australia, which can be changed based on the requirement.

CATALOGUE SEARCHING

Details about a book or any other library material can be searched by either item number or by a combination of fields such as keywords, title, author, Dewey classification number, class (fiction, CD ROM, etc., or by subject. The search can be either normal or exact search. If any matches are available, the search results are displayed, which include title, author, copyright, number of copies available in the library, the transaction details, i.e. if the book is borrowed or reserved or available on the shelf details can be got. If the user has to borrow a particular book, then one can do that by clicking on the request button.

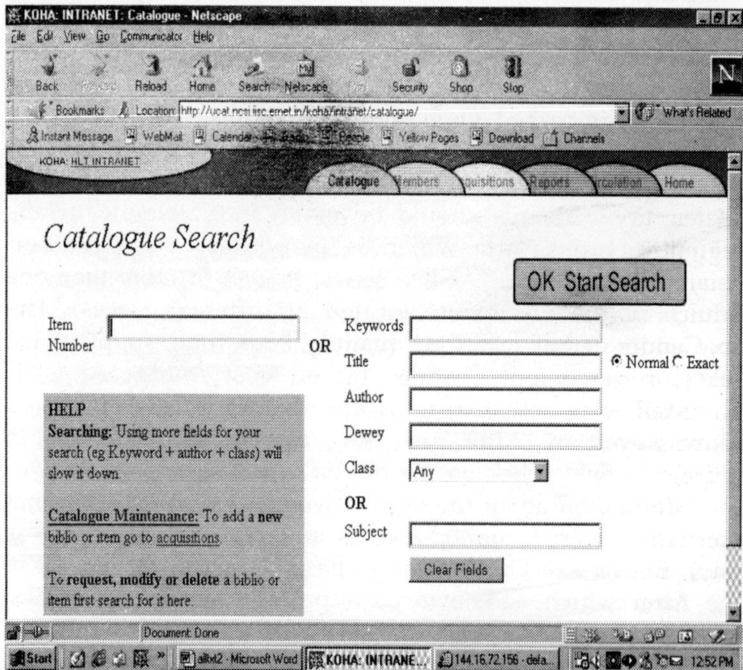

MEMBER MODULE

Search facilitates to renew items, view addresses, modify and delete records. Type a borrower name, part of a name, or number in this field and hit the enter key to activate search. The member module of koha maintain member's record containing detail such as name, address, telephone, fax, email membership number, card number, Card Category, Address, OD/Issues, Fines notes, etc.

Using this function a new member can be added. We can add adult or institution by using this option.

ADDING AN ADULT MEMBER

Member ID

This is the identification number of a member. It may be numerical or a combination of alphabets and numbers. The length of this mandatory field is 10 characters and it is generated by the system.

Member Card Number: This is the member card number, which may be numeric or a combination of both the alphabets and numbers. The length is of 9 characters and it is generated by system. This is also a mandatory field.

Member personal detail: Here personal information related to a member such as Gender, Date of birth, name beginning with 'Title', initial, name, surname, Ethnicity (i.e. Asian, Indian), Ethnicity Notes, Membership Category (i.e. Adult, Privileged) is given which is defined in the system set-up. Gender surname and Membership Category are mandatory field, for arranging the entries in the order.

Mailing Address: This field is mandatory. It is the postal address and town. It could either be residential or office address.

Member contact detail: There is provision to enter alternative phone numbers such as Phone (Home), Phone (day), Email, Fax.

Alternative contact Details: It is optional. One might enter residential/permanent address here in our friend or work place. Category is mandatory field.

Registration Date: This is usually the system date the time of membership registration.

Membership Expiry date: The expiry date of the registration is determined by the System.

Category: A valid category as defined in the system set-up. It is mandatory field and determines the borrowing privileges of the member.

Access level: User defined one character level to specify the privileges of the member to access the database/document

Library Use: You can write notes related to a member to indicate if he/she is active user or some time visitor.

FORMAT II FOR INSTITUTION MEMBER

Institution details: An institution member type institution name.

Institution Address: This field is mandatory. It is the mailing address, either the institution of residential address.

Contact Details: This field includes the name, phone, fax and e-mail and notes. Name and the mandatory field.

Registration Date: This is usually the system date the time of membership registration.

Membership Expiry date: The expiry date of the registration is determined by the System.

Category: A valid category as defined in the system set-up. It is mandatory field and determines the borrowing privileges of the member.

Access level: User defined one character level to specify the privileges of the member to access the database/document.

Library Use: You can write notes related to a member. He may an active user or some time only a visitor. Any specific remark can be entered here as notes.

Membership Record: The record has all information related to member we can see all the information such as membership number, postal address, Home address, phone (daytime), phone (home) telephone No., Fax, membership number, category, area, join date, expires date, alternative contact detail, name, phone, etc.

Modify: This is used to change the details of a existing record on selection of this option the one the records is opened the system displays the details and accepts change click save change system accepts the member ID whose record is to be modified.

Delete Record: In case duplication records are creating for a member (obviously with different Ids) the records created later may be removed through this function.

Note: Removed member records are taken out from the database permanently.

ADD CHILD

This option is used to add new child member up on selecting this option the system either asks for a member card No. here we can Add New Junior Member.

Following Fields are Available :

Parent or Guardian: The system automatic taken parent or guardian information such as Title, Given Names, Surname, and Membership No.

Child 1: There is provision to enter Given name, Surname, Card No. Gender (M or F), Date of Birth, school, here all mandatory field except school.

Child 2: There is provision to enter Given name, Surname, Card No. Gender (M or F), Date of Birth, school, here all mandatory field except school

Child 3: There is provision to enter Given name, Surname, Card No. Gender (M or F), Date of Birth, school, here all mandatory field except school

Fines $ Charges: Fines are computed for delayed checking-in or renewal of document and this is noted/posted in the member's record. Subsequent recording of fine collection is based on member ID. Amount due as fine from the member is displayed by the system. This function used to collect payment from a member whose fine amount has been computed while he checked-in or renewal the document. We can see here view account and we can change pay change.

Following Key Options are Available:

- Unpaid
- Pay
- Write-off

Items Current on Issue: The lists of document, which have been Issued for user, it includes document title, due date, Item type, charge, renew. Here we can renew document for users.

Items Requesting: The list of documents, which have been reserved by member. System displays some field such as title, Requested Date, Charge, Remove. When you are click title, it includes all information regarding reserve book.

Reading Record: This option show list of document, which has been, rode by barrowers it includes, title, author, document return date, and Volume No.

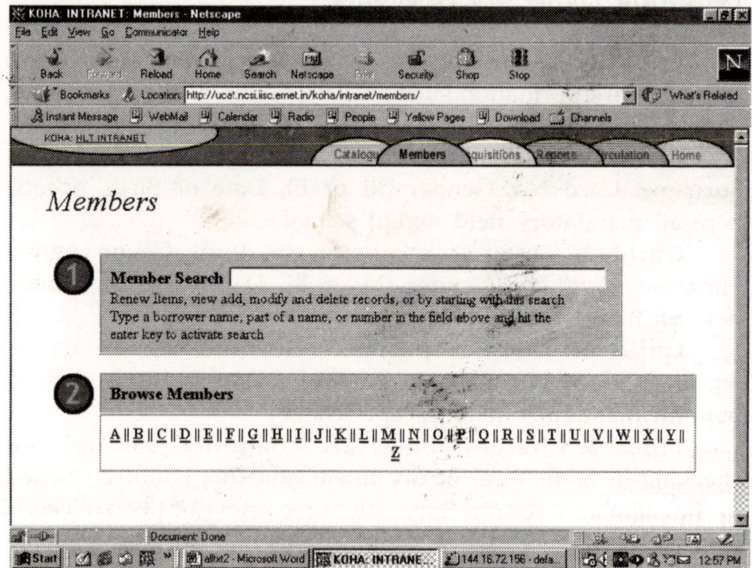

REPORT MODULE

This is complete list of members who have been charged

an amount of fine totally individual fines, of which payment has been made only in past. The outstanding amount is listed in the fine payment column.

Fine List: this is of fines charged by the library. On selection of the option the system prints the member's name, category, due date and the amount charged is available date-wise.

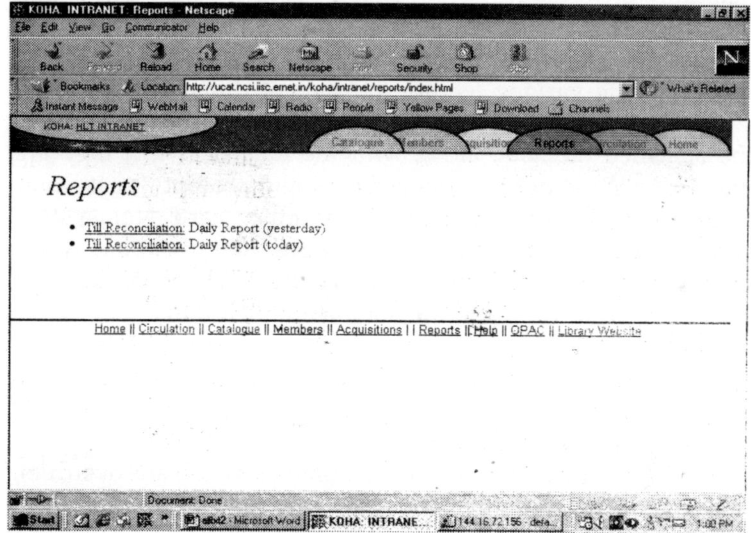

CIRCULATION MODULE

The circulation system maintains up to date membership record and the latest status of the collection meant for circulation. It supports all the functions related to circulation providing suitable check at every stage. It takes care of infrequent but routine functions such as bindery record management, display recent addition and so on. The purpose of this module of the circulation module is to control and rapidly process all loan and other circulation transactions.

Checkout: While issuing a book the respective user's last name or member card number is keyed in the place provided in circulation section. This takes to the issuing form which includes the item number box, if entered gives the status of that particular book i.e., if it is available in the library or is it been issued and to whom it is issued to which branch and what is the due date. If there is any fine/charge need to be paid by the user to the library, then book will not get issued to that user until he will clear all dues. If some member has reserved a book andwhen it comes back will not be renewed to the same member. This function involves entering either manually or wending the bar-coded Member card number and the item barcode of the documents being checked-out the system provides flexibility (through the set-up parameters) to accommodate varying lending policies of different library.

The gives the list of document currently checked-out by the specified member, along with the date on witch they are due on selection of this option the system prompt one to enter a member ID. On entering the member card No. system display the member name card status and the date witch membership expires. It also displays the count of outstanding documents due from the member with such detail.

- Check-out (number of the library document checked-out).
- Last date of check-out.
- Overdue (number of documents witch are overdue).
- Recalls (number of titles which have been recall from the member but are still pending).
- Reserve (the number of titles reserved by the number).

While checking out patron information is given which briefs about the member ID, his last name, and his department address along with the category. If the member has any flags against him or any overdue charges it is highlighted.

There is option for sticky due date, which strictly looks for the due date.

Check in: Check in of the book is known as Returns in Koha, if any issued book is returned on or after due date, the item number is keyed in, which provides the details about the book as well as the member information. It involves entering either manually or wending the bar-coded accession No. of the document being check-in. While checking-in a document may be reported as damaged or lost there is the option to compute fines for delayed check-in.

Require: When a member enquires about the status of the title he has reserved this facility is used. On selection of the Require the system asks for member card No. on entering the same, the system display such detail as the name of the member list of the current along with the priority sequence of each. Two prompt appear at the bottom of the screen.

Overdue Notice: The over due notice are generated by having any document monograph, journals or documents on lone under ILL that have not been returned long past the due date, there is a facility to include the address so that notices may be maintain directly to members optionally, along with overdue titles may generated for the record of the library staff.

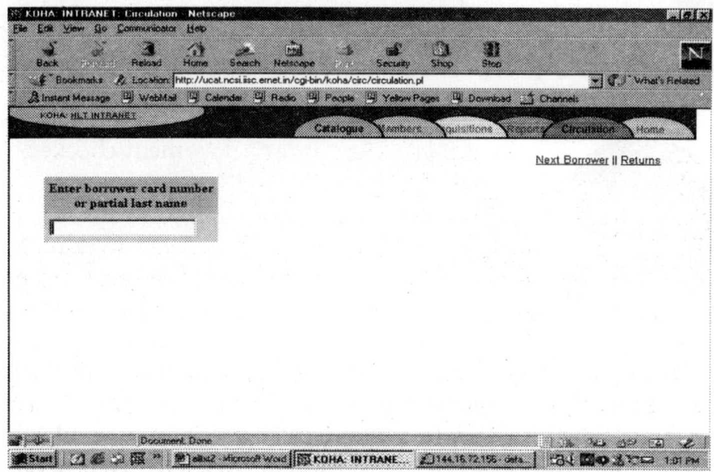

OPAC (ONLINE PUBLIC ACCESSIBLE CATALOGUE)

The OPAC module usually comes with some default OPAC that can be used as a starter. Most libraries will prefer to take the opportunity to tailor the OPAC to their specific library, and there is usually provision for individual library OPAC design. The library can identify and design specific menus for staff and public use; dialogues and messages can be defined, as can any information and help texts. Help is normally context-specific so that an appropriate message can be displayed in accordance with the stage that has been reached in the search.

In Koha, the OPAC is made very simple and the user can do only simple search. The OPAC frame has provision for searching title, keywords, author, subject, class or document type and item number. In this software there is no option for advanced search such as Boolean search.

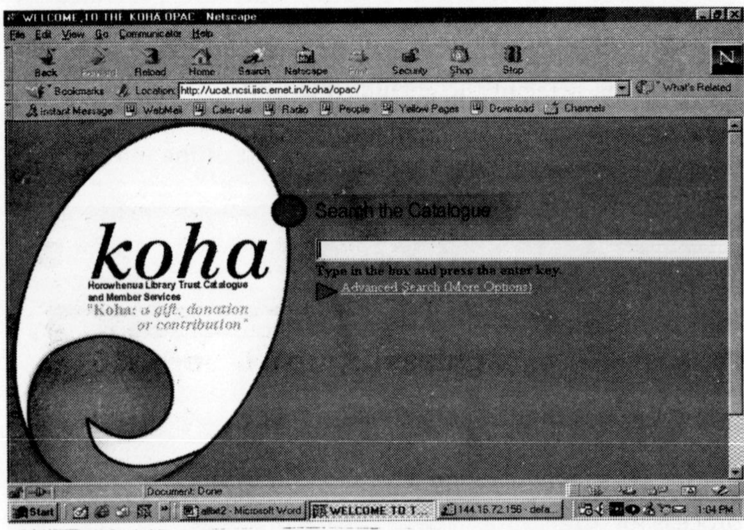

Being a Koha freeware, any Library wanting to automate their library house keeping operations can make use of this software's however, this freeware is at present is available for LINUX and Windows operating System, MYSQL, Web server administrative this s/w is ideal for all schools, College Libraries, Public Libraries.

6

Digital Library

A digital library is a library in which a significant proportion of the resources are available in machine-readable format (as opposed to print or microform), accessible by means of computers. The digital content may be locally held or accessed remotely via computer networks. In libraries, the process of digitization began with the catalog, moved to periodical indexes and abstracting services, then to periodicals and large reference works, and finally to book publishing. Some of the largest digital libraries are purely digital having few if any physical holdings.

DEFINING DIGITAL LIBRARIES

Digital libraries are defined in many ways, encompassing both analog materials made available digitally and newly created digital content. Already there is misconception about digital libraries in the minds of some people, particularly traditional library professionals. Because of lack of understanding of the fundamental concepts, different things mean to different people. Some still feel that on-line catalogues or bibliographies are 'digital' resources. It should be noted that these electronic resources are only 'pointers' to documents and do not constitute the 'content' or full-text of documents. With so much of ongoing research in the area of digital libraries, problems of terminology, standards, and quality are bound to crop up.

Under these circumstances, we need to have a clear idea of the concepts, technologies, standards, formats, protocols, policies and legal/ethical issues, before venturing into digital libraries. "The future of digital library history will be determined not by the technology involved, but by the ideology. If the prevailing definition of a digital library is an organized searchable collection in digital format, then the future of digital libraries will reflect a move toward integrated service functions and collection development and management similar to the traditional library organization".

TYPES OF DIGITAL LIBRARIES

The term digital library is diffuse enough to be applicable to a wide range of digital entities. Divisions can be made between libraries that have some physical presence, where patrons are able to access physical holdings as well as digital holdings and libraries where collections are almost completely digital. Project Gutenberg, Bibiblio, and the Internet Archive can serve as examples of this later case.

ADVANTAGES

Traditional libraries are limited by storage space; digital libraries have the potential to store much more information, simply because digital information requires very little physical space to contain it. As such, the cost of maintaining a digital library is much lower than that of a traditional library. A traditional library must spend large sums of money paying for staff, book maintenance, rent, and additional books. Digital libraries do away with these fees.

Digital libraries can immediately adopt innovations in technology providing users with improvements in electronic and audio book technology as well as presenting new forms of communication such as wikis and blogs.

No Physical Boundary

The user of a digital library need not to go to the library physically; people from all over the world can gain access to the same information, as long as an Internet connection is available.

Round the Clock Availability

A major advantage of digital libraries is that people can gain access to the information at any time, night or day.

Multiple Accesses

The same resources can be used at the same time by a number of users.

Structured Approach

Digital libraries provide access to much richer content in a more structured manner, i.e. we can easily move from the catalog to the particular book then to a particular chapter and so on.

Information Retrieval

The user is able to use any search term bellowing to the word or phrase of the entire collection. Digital libraries can provide very user-friendly interfaces, giving clickable access to its resources.

Preservation and Conservation

An exact copy of the original can be made any number of times without any degradation in quality.

Space

Whereas traditional libraries are limited by storage space, digital libraries have the potential to store much more information, simply because digital information requires very little physical space to contain them. When a library has no space for extension digitization is the only solution.

Networking

A particular digital library can provide a link to any other resources of other digital libraries very easily; thus a seamlessly integrated resource sharing can be achieved.

Cost

In theory, the cost of maintaining a digital library is lower than that of a traditional library. A traditional library must spend large sums of money paying for staff, book maintenance, rent, and additional books. Although digital libraries do away with these fees, it has since been found that digital libraries can be no less expensive in their own way to operate. Digital libraries can and do incur large costs for the conversion of print materials into digital format, for the technical skills of staff to maintain them, and for the costs of maintaining online access (i.e servers, bandwidth costs, etc.). Also, the information in a digital library must often be "migrated" every few years to the latest digital media. This process can incur very large costs in hardware and skilled personnel. (See data migration).

PROBLEMS

Some people have criticized that digital libraries are hampered by copyright law, because works cannot be shared over different periods of time in the manner of a traditional library. The content is, in many cases, public domain or self-generated content only. Some digital libraries, such as Project Gutenberg, work to digitize out-of-copyright works and make them freely available to the public. An estimate of the number of distinct books still existent in library catalogues from 2000B.C. to 1960, has been made.

- Other digital libraries (more specifically, digitial collections, which may be acquired by libraries) accommodate copyright concerns by licensing content and distributing it on a commercial basis, which allows for better management of the content's reproduction and the payment (if required) of royalties.
- Digital libraries cannot reproduce the environment of a traditional library. Many people also find reading printed material to be easier than reading material on a computer screen although this depends heavily on presentation as well as personal preferences. Also, due to technological developments, a digital library can see some of its content become out-of-date and its data may become unaccessible.
- Access to digital libraries and their collections is dependent upon a stable information technology infrastructure (power, computers, communications links, etc.). Hence, despite the egalitarian potential of the digitial library, many of those who could most benefit from its global reach (for instance in the Third World) are not able to do so.

ACADEMIC REPOSITORIES

Many academic libraries are actively involved in building institutional repositories of the institution's books, papers, theses, and other works which can be digitized. Many of these repositories are made available to the academic community or, sadly for the true aims of societal non-profits, only rarely, the general public. Insitutional, truly free, and corporate repositories are often referred to as digital libraries.

ELECTRONIC RESOURCES IN DIGITAL LIBRARIES

- Electronic Library is made up of different online resources from various vendors, which may include: EBSCO, Gale, OCLC Collection, ProQuest, and netLibrary.

EBSCO

Academic Search™ Premier contains indexing for nearly 8,050 publications, with full text for more than 4,600 of those titles. PDF backfiles to 1975 or further are available for well over one hundred journals, and searchable references are provided for more than 1,000 titles. Academic Search Premier contains full text coverage in biology, chemistry, education, engineering, humanities, physics, psychology, religion and theology, sociology, etc.

Business Source® Premier offers indexing and abstracts for the 350 scholarly journals back to 1965 or the first published issue. This database includes searchable references for more than 1,170 journals. Journal ranking studies reveal that Business Source Premier is an excellent database for full text journals in all disciplines of business, including marketing, management, Marketing of Information System, Principles of Management, accounting, finance, econometrics and economics.

Regional Business News™. A supplemental database for customers of Business Source Premier. With daily updates, Regional Business News provides comprehensive full text for regional business publications (including titles from Crain Communications). Regional Business News has full text for more than 60 sources.

MasterFILE™ Premier contains full text for 2,053 periodicals covering general reference, business, health, education, general science, multicultural issues and much more. This database also contains full text for more than 350 reference books, 84,074 biographies, 86,132 primary source documents, and an Image Collection of 107,135 photos, maps & flags. MasterFILE Premier now offers PDF backfiles (as far back as 1975) for key publications including American Libraries, Foreign Affairs, History Today, Judaism, Library Journal, National Review, Saturday Evening Post, etc.

OCLC COLLECTION

WorldCat (The OCLC Online Union Catalog). (Approximately 2100 B.C.—present; Updated daily)

The world's most comprehensive bibliography, with more than 50 million bibliographic records representing 400 languages. Covers information back to 2100 B.C. Includes holdings information from libraries across the world. Bibliographic information only.

Electronic Collections Online. Access citations only from the full-image articles from Electronic Collections Online journals. Full-text/image articles from selected journals are available to their special group only.

PROQUEST

ProQuest Newspapers is an accessible and thorough Web-based database with citations and abstracts from over 350 newspapers, over 250 of which provide full text, enabling users to search the latest news from around the world.

Coverage, updated daily, of local, state, regional, national, and international newspapers is available, including full-text access to 27 major newspapers: the Star Tribune, The Wall Street Journal, The Washington Post, The New York Times, the Chicago Tribune, the Los Angeles Times, Barron's, and USA Today, to name just a few. One can access a wide range of articles, not only top news stories, but arts, sports, and entertainment stories as well.

MINITEX

The MINITEX Library Information Network is a publicly supported network of libraries in Minnesota, North Dakota, and South Dakota working cooperatively to improve library service.

MINITEX's mission is to enhance the effectiveness and efficiency of participating libraries by expanding their access to local, state, regional, national, and international information resources through conventional and innovative means.

MNLINK GATEWAY

The MnLINK Gateway is a World Wide Web-based virtual library, providing access to multiple information resources, including open access to participating Minnesota library catalogs and secured access to available electronic databases. In addition, the MnLINK Gateway provides links to selected free Internet resources. Click here to learn more about MnLINK.

ELECTRONIC RESOURCES—META DATA, META DATA STANDARDS

The exponential growth of interest in the Internet in recent years has created a digital extension of the academic research library for certain kinds of materials. Valuable collections of texts, images and sounds from many scholarly communities — collections that may even be the subject of state-of-the-art discussions in these communities—now exist only in electronic form and may be accessible from the Internet. Knowledge regarding the whereabouts and status of this material is often passed on by word of mouth among members of a given community. For outsiders, however, much of this material is so difficult to locate that it is effectively unavailable.

WHAT IS METADATA?

Metadata is structured information that describes, explains, locates, or otherwise makes it easier to retrieve, use or manage an information resource. Metadata is often called data about data or information about information. The term metadata is used differently in different communities. Some use it to refer to machine understandable information, while others use it only for records that describe electronic resources. However, in the library environment, metadata is commonly used for any formal scheme of resource description, applying to any type of object, digital or non-digital. Traditional library cataloging is a form of metadata, and MARC 21 and the rule sets used with it such as AACR2 are metadata standards.

Other metadata schemes have been developed to describe various types of textual and non-textual objects such as archival materials, visual materials, geographic information, and science and social science datasets. There are several different types of metadata, including descriptive, administrative, and structural. Descriptive metadata describes a resource for purposes such as discovery and identification. It can include elements such as title, abstract, author, and keywords. Administrative metadata provides information to help manage a resource, such as when and how it was created, file type and other technical information, and who can access it. Rights management metadata is a form of administrative metadata dealing with intellectual property rights. Structural metadata indicates how compound objects are put together, for example, how pages are ordered to form chapters.

Metadata can describe resources at any level of aggregation. It can describe a collection, a unitary resource, or a component part of a larger resource (for example, a photograph in an article). Just as catalogers make decisions about whether a catalog record should be created for a whole set of volumes or for each particular volume in the set, so the metadata creator makes similar decisions. Metadata can also be used for description at any level of the information model laid out in the IFLA (International Federation of Library Associations and Institutions), Functional Requirements for Bibliographic Records (http://www.ifla.org/VII/s13/frbr/frbr.pdf): work, expression, manifestation, or item. For example, a metadata record could describe a report, a particular edition of the report, or a specific copy of that edition of the report.

Metadata can be embedded in a digital object or it can be stored separately. Metadata is often embedded in HTML documents and in the headers of image files. Storing metadata with the object it describes ensures the metadata will not be lost, obviates problems of linking between data and metadata, and helps ensure that the metadata and object will be updated together. However, it is impossible to embed metadata in some types of objects (for example, artifacts). Also, storing metadata separately can simplify the management of the metadata itself and facilitate search and retrieval. Therefore, metadata is commonly stored in database systems and linked to the objects described.

Metadata schemes (also called schema) are sets of metadata elements designed for a particular purpose, for example, to describe a particular type of information resource. The definition or meaning of the elements themselves is known as the semantics of the scheme. The values given to metadata elements are the content. Metadata schemes generally specify names of elements and their semantics. Optionally, they may specify content rules for how content must be formulated (for example, how to identify the main title) and/or representation rules for how content must be represented (for example, capitalization rules). There may also be syntax rules for how the elements and their content should be encoded.

A metadata scheme with no prescribed syntax rules is called syntax independent. Metadata can be encoded in MARC, in "keyword=value" pairs, or in any other definable syntax. Many current metadata schemes use SGML or XML. XML (Extensible Mark-up Language) is an extended form of HTML which allows for locally defined tag sets and the easy exchange of structured information. SGML (Standard Generalized Mark-up Language) is a superset of both HTML and XML and allows for the richest mark-up of a document.

WHAT DOES METADATA DO?

An important reason for creating descriptive metadata is to facilitate discovery of relevant information. In addition to resource discovery, metadata can help organize electronic resources, facilitate interoperability and legacy resource integration, support digital identification, and support archiving and preservation.

METADATA ELEMENT SETS

Resource Discovery

Identification of information is known as resource identification. Today in the semantic web environment, information is treated as objects. In this context resource identification comes to be known as Resource Discovery.

Metadata serves the same functions in resource discovery as good cataloging does by:

- allowing resources to be found by relevant criteria;
- identifying resources;
- bringing similar resources together;
- distinguishing dissimilar resources;
- giving location information.

ORGANIZING ELECTRONIC RESOURCES

As the number of Web-based resources grows exponentially, aggregate items or portals are increasingly useful in organizing links to resources based on audience or topic. Such lists can be built as static web pages, with the names and locations of the resources "hard coded" in the HTML. However, it is more efficient and increasingly more common to build these pages dynamically from metadata stored in databases. Software tools such as ColdFusion® can be used to automatically extract and reformat the information for web applications (http://www.allaire.com/Products/coldfusion/).

Another method of organizing Web information is through channels. Channels are preselected Web sites that automatically "push" streams of information to a user's browser, commonly used for continuously updated information such as stock quotes and news. The dominant metadata scheme for web casting is the Channel Definition Format (CDF) developed by Microsoft and its partners (http://www.w3.org/TR/NOTE-CDFsubmit.html, http://msdn.microsoft.com/workshop/delivery/cdf /reference/CDF.asp).

INTEROPERABILITY

Describing a resource with metadata allows it to be understood by both humans and machines in ways that promote interoperability. Interoperability is the ability of multiple systems, with different hardware and software platforms, data structures, and interfaces, to exchange data with minimal loss of content and functionality. Using defined metadata schemes, shared transfer protocols, and crosswalks between schemes, resources across the network can be searched more seamlessly.

Two approaches to interoperability are cross-system search and metadata harvesting. The Z39.50 protocol is commonly used for cross system search (http://www.loc.gov/z3950/agency/). Z39.50 partners do not share metadata but map their own search capabilities to a common set of search attributes. A contrasting approach taken by the Open Archives Initiative (http://www.openarchives.org) is for all partners to translate their native metadata to a common core set of elements and expose this for harvesting. A search service then gathers the metadata into a consistent central index to allow cross-repository searching regardless of the metadata formats used by participating repositories.

DIGITAL IDENTIFICATION

Most metadata schemes include elements such as standard numbers to uniquely identify the work or object to which the metadata refers. The location of a digital object may also be given using a file name, URL, or some more persistent identifier such as a Persistent URL (PURL) or the **Digital Object Identifier** (DOI).

Persistent identifiers are preferred because file locations change frequently, making the URL (and therefore the metadata record) invalid. In addition to the actual elements that point to the object, the metadata can be combined to act as a set of identifying data, differentiating one object from another for validation purposes.

ARCHIVING AND PRESERVATION

Most current metadata efforts center around the discovery of recently created resources. However, there is a growing concern that digital resources will not survive in usable form into the future. Digital information is fragile; it can be corrupted or altered, intentionally or unintentionally. It may become unusable as storage media and hardware and software technologies change.

Format migration and perhaps emulation of current hardware and software behavior in future hardware and software platforms are strategies for overcoming these challenges.

Metadata is the key to ensuring that resources will survive and continue to be accessible into the future. Archiving and preservation require special elements to track the lineage of a digital object (where it came from and how it has changed over time), to detail its physical characteristics, and to document its behavior in order to emulate it on future technologies.

Many organizations internationally are working on defining metadata schemes for digital preservation, including the National Library of Australia (http://www.nla.gov.au/padi/topics/32.html), the British Cedars Project (CURL Exemplars in Digital Archives) (http://www.leeds.ac.uk/cedars/metadata.html), and a joint Working Group of OCLC and the Research Libraries Group (RLG) (http://www.oclc.org/digitalpreservation/presmeta_wp.pdf). Many of these initiatives are based on or compatible with the ISO Reference Model for an Open Archival Information System (OAIS) which incorporates preservation metadata along with descriptive, administrative, and rights management metadata (http://www.ccsds org/RP9905/RP9905.html).

Metadata Element Sets Used in Library Environments

Many different metadata schemes are being used in library environments. A few of the most common ones are mentioned below.

- Marc 21
- Dublin Core
- Global (Government) Information Locator Service (GILS)
- Text Encoding Initiative (TEI) Header
- Encoded Archival Description
- Visual Resources Association (VRA) Core Categories

MARC 21 Concise Bibliographic: Introduction

The MARC 21 Format for Bibliographic Data is designed to be a carrier for bibliographic information about printed and manuscript textual materials, computer files, maps, music, continuing resources, visual materials, and mixed materials. Bibliographic data commonly includes titles, names, subjects, notes, publication data, and information about the physical description of an item. The bibliographic format contains data elements for the following types of material:

Books—Textual material that is monographic in nature.

Continuing Resources—Textual items with a recurring pattern of publication, e.g., periodicals, newspapers, yearbooks. (*Note:* Prior to 2002, continuing resources were referred to as serials.)

Computer Files—Used for computer software, numeric data, computer-oriented multimedia, online systems or services. Other classes of electronic resources are coded for their most significant aspect. Material may be monographic or serial in nature.

Maps—All types of cartographic materials, including sheet maps and globes in printed, manuscript, electronic, and microform.

Music—Printed and manuscript notated music.

Sound Recordings—Nonmusical sound recordings, and musical sound recordings.

Visual Materials—Projected media, two-dimensional graphics, three-dimensional artifacts or naturally occurring objects, and kits. Used for archival visual materials when format or medium is being emphasized.

Mixed Materials—Primarily archival and manuscript collections of a mixture of forms of material. Material may be monographic or serial in nature.

KINDS OF BIBLIOGRAPHIC RECORDS

MARC bibliographic records are distinguished from all other types of MARC records by specific codes in Leader/06 (Type of record) which identifies the following bibliographic record types.

Language (textual) material	Nonmusical sound recording
Manuscript language (textual) material	Musical sound recording
Computer file	Projected medium
Cartographic material	Two-dimensional non-projectable graphic
Manuscript cartographic material	Three-dimensional artifact or natural objects
Notated music	Kit
Manuscript music	Mixed material

FILL CHARACTER

A fill character (hexadecimal value '7C'), represented in this document and ASCII as a vertical bar (|), may be used in bibliographic records in some positions in fields 006, 007 and 008, and subfield $7 of the linking entry fields (760-787). A fill character may not be used anywhere in the leader, or in tags, indicators, or subfield codes. The use of the fill character in records contributed to a national database may also be dependent upon the national level requirements specified for each data element. The presence of a fill character in a bibliographic record indicates that the format specifies a code to be used but the creator of the record has decided not to attempt to supply a code.

TYPOGRAPHICAL CONVENTIONS

Throughout this document, the following typographical conventions are used:

0 — The graphic 0 represents the digit zero in tags, fixed-position character position citations, and indicator positions. This character is distinct from an uppercase letter O used in examples or text.

— The graphic symbol # is used for a blank (hex 20) in coded fields and in other special situations where the existence of the character blank might be ambiguous.

$ — The graphic symbol $ is used for the delimiter (hex 1F) portion of a subfield code. Within the text, subfield codes are referred to as *subfield $a,* for example.

/— Specific character positions of fixed-length data elements, such as those in the Leader, Directory, and field 008, are expressed using a slash and the number of the character position, e.g., Leader/06.

1 — The graphic 1 represents the digit one (hex 31). This character must be distinguished from a lowercase roman alphabet letter l (el) (hex 6C) and the uppercase alphabetic letter I (eye) (hex 49) in examples or text.

| — The graphic | represents a fill character (hex 7C).

DUBLIN CORE

The Dublin Core Metadata Element Set arose from discussions at a 1995 workshop sponsored by OCLC and the National Center for Supercomputing Applications (NCSA). As the workshop was held in Dublin, Ohio, the element set was named the Dublin Core. The continuing development of the Dublin Core and related specifications is managed by the Dublin Core Metadata Initiative (DCMI) (http://dublincore.org/). The original objective of the Dublin Core was to define a set of elements that could be used by authors to describe their own Web resources. Faced with a proliferation of electronic resources and the inability of the library profession to catalog all these resources, the goal was to define a few elements and some simple rules that could be applied by noncatalogers.

The original 13 core elements were later increased to 15:

- title,
- subject,
- description,
- source,
- language,
- relation,

- coverage,
- creator,
- publisher,
- contributor,
- rights,
- date,
- type,
- format, and
- identifier.

To make this discussion concrete, consider an electronic a record created with the relevant portions of the Dublin Core, and a sample syntax, that describes an electronic version of Maya Angelou's poem "On the Pulse of Morning". This description is based on a record created by the University of Virginia Library's Electronic Text Center.

- **Subject:** Poetry
- **Title:** On the Pulse of Morning
- **Creator:** Maya Angelou
- **Publisher:** University of Virgina Library Electronic Text Center
- **Other Agent:** Transcribed by the University of Virginia Electronic Text Center
- **Date:** 1993
- **Object:** Poem
- **Form:** 1 ASCII file
- **Identifier:** AngPuls1
- **Source:** Newspaper stories and oral performance of text at the presidential inauguration of Bill Clinton
- **Language:** English

The Dublin Core was developed to be simple and concise, and to describe Web-based documents. However, Dublin Core has been used with other types of materials and in applications demanding some complexity

GREENSTONE

Greenstone is a suite of software for building and

distributing digital library collections. It provides a new way of organizing information and publishing it on the Internet or on CD-ROM. Greenstone is produced by the New Zealand Digital Library Project at the University of Waikato, and developed and distributed in cooperation with UNESCO and the Human Info NGO. It is open-source, multilingual software, issued under the terms of the GNU General Public License. Read the Greenstone Fact Sheet for more information.

The aim of the Greenstone software is to empower users, particularly in universities, libraries, and other public service institutions, to build their own digital libraries. Digital libraries are radically reforming how information is disseminated and acquired in UNESCO's partner communities and institutions in the fields of education, science and culture around the world, and particularly in developing countries. We hope that this software will encourage the effective deployment of digital libraries to share information and place it in the public domain.

TECHNICAL

Platforms

Greenstone runs on all versions of Windows, and UNIX, and Mac OS-X. It is very easy to install. For the default Windows installation absolutely no configuration is necessary, and end users routinely install Greenstone on their personal laptops or workstations. Institutional users run it on their main web server, where it interoperates with standard web server software (e.g. Apache).

Interoperability

Greenstone is highly interoperable using contemporary standards, It incorporates a server that can serve any collection over the Open Archives Protocol for Metadata Harvesting (OAI-PMH), and Greenstone can harvest documents over OAI-PMH and include them in a collection. Any collection can be exported to METS (in the Greenstone METS Profile, approved by the METS Editorial Board and published at http://www.loc.gov/standards/mets/mets-profiles.html), and Greenstone can ingest documents in METS form. Any collection can be exported to DSpace ready for DSpace's batch import program, and any DSpace collection can be imported into Greenstone.

Interfaces. Greenstone has two separate interactive interfaces, the Reader interface and the Librarian interface. End users access the digital library through the Reader interface, which operates within a web browser. The Librarian interface is a Java-based graphical user interface (also available as an applet) that makes it easy to gather material for a collection (downloading it from the web where necessary), enrich it by adding metadata, design the searching and browsing facilities that the collection will offer the user, and build and serve the collection.

Metadata formats. Users define metadata interactively within the Librarian interface. These metadata sets are predefined:

- Dublin Core (qualified and unqualified).
- RFC 1807.
- NZGLS (New Zealand Government Locator Service).
- AGLS (Australian Government Locator Service).

New metadata sets can be defined using Greenstone's Metadata Set Editor. "Plug-ins" are used to ingest externally-prepared metadata in different forms, and plug-ins exist for

- XML, MARC, CDS/ISIS, ProCite, BibTex, Refer, OAI, DSpace, METS

Document formats. Plug-ins are also used to ingest documents. For textual documents, there is plug-ins for

- PDF, PostScript, Word, RTF, HTML, Plain text, Latex, ZIP archives, Excel, PPT, Email (various formats), source code

For multimedia documents, there are plug-ins for :

- Images (any format, including GIF, JIF, JPEG, TIFF), MP3 audio, Ogg Vorbis audio, and a generic plug-in that can be configured for audio formats, MPEG, MIDI, etc.

USER BASE

Distribution. As with all open source projects, the user base for Greenstone is unknown. It is distributed on SourceForge, a leading distribution centre for open source software.

Distributed via Source Forge since:	Nov 2000
Average downloads since then:	4500/month
Currently running at:	4500/month
Proportion of downloads that are documentation:	60%
Proportion of downloads that are software:	40%

Of these, 80% are Windows binaries 15% are Linux binaries 5% are source.

Examples. Examples of public Greenstone collections (see http://www.greenstone.org for URLs) can be found at:

- Association of Indian Labour Historians, Delhi
- Auburn University, Alabama
- California University at Riverside
- Chicago University Library
- Detroit Public Library
- Gresham College, London
- Hawaiian Electronic Library
- Illinois Wesleyan University
- Indian Institute of Management
- Kyrgyz Republic National Library
- LeHigh University, Pennsylvania
- Mari El Republic, Russia
- National Centre for Science Information, Bangalore, India
- Netherlands Institute for Scientific Information Services

- New York Botanical Garden
- Peking University Digital Library
- Philippine Research Education and Government Information Network
- Slavonski Brod Public Library, Slovenia
- State Library of Tasmania
- Stuttgart University of Applied Sciences
- Texas A&M University Center for the Study of Digital Libraries
- University of Illinois
- Vietnam National University
- Vimercate Public Library, Milan, Italy
- Washington Research Library Consortium
- Welsh Books Council

UN agencies with an interest in Greenstone include—

- UNESCO, Paris
- Sponsors distribution of the Greenstone software as part of its Information for All programme
- Food and Agriculture Organization (FAO), Rome
- The Information Management Resource Kit uses Greenstone as the (only) example of digital library software in the Digitization and Digital Libraries self-instructional module
- Institute for Information Technology in Education (IITE), Moscow
    - o Have commissioned an extensive course on Digital libraries in education that uses Greenstone for all the practical work
    - o United Nations University (UNU), Japan
    - o Two CD-ROM collections of UNU material have been produced

Humanitarian collections. Greenstone is used by Human Info NGO in Belgium to produced collections of humanitarian information and distribute them on CD-ROM widely throughout the developing world. (For more information, contact Michel Loots mloots@humaninfo.org)

Number of humanitarian collections: approx 35-40
Annual distribution of each one: approx 5,000 copies

Languages. One of Greenstone's unique strengths is its multilingual nature. The reader's interface is available in the following languages:

- Arabic, Armenian, Bengali, Catalan, Croatian, Czech, Chinese (both simplified and traditional), Dutch, English, Farsi, Finnish, French, Galician, Georgian, German, Greek, Hebrew, Hindi, Indonesian, Italian, Japanese, Kannada, Kazakh, Kyrgyz, Latvian, Maori, Mongolian, Portuguese (BR and PT versions), Russian, Serbian, Spanish, Thai, Turkish, Ukrainian, Vietnamese.

  E-prints (http://www.eprints.org/software/)

E-print Open Archives Software to building collection for open access to all. Digital libraries were initiated in response to the need for organized management of networked information services in a distributed environment where both the users and resources are at varied locations. EPrints archive Software can be used to create online collections of research papers, preprints; post prints and so on, and was initially developed at the School of Electronics and Computer Science, University of Southampton, UK. The software used for developing digital libraries, then can come form a variety of organizations or form an open source collection. This portal in one of the interface to a digital library as the means by which used interacts with the information collection, has crucial role to play. An Institutional Repository is the best way to provide Open Access to research output. The growing impact of IT has somehow completed librarian to use IT effectively to render service and with the growing number of open archives, it has become imperative for information professionals to redefine the process of collection development.

Indian Institute of Science, Bangalore, India (21203 records)

Indian Institute of Science, Bangalore, India (21203 records)
NAL-IR (3078 records)
OpenMED@NIC (2445 records http://openmed.nic.in/
EPrints@IIT Delhi : Home (2154 records)
National Centre for Catalysis Research (IIT): Catalysis Database (1293 records)
http://203.199.213.48/
DU Eprint Archive (178 records)
http://eprints.du.ac.in/

Fedora (http://www.fedora.info)

The Flexible Extensible Digital Object and Repository Architecture originates with Cornell's Digital Library Research Group, and the current system is maintained in partnership with he University of Virginia, using funding form the Andrew M. Mellon Foundation. Fedora was released as an open source project in mid-2003 and represents a sophisticated and mature architecture for storing digital objects. Fedora has adopted METS to manage objects as XML entities and exposes digital objects through a persistent ID (PID) so that they can be referenced in URLs. Object-related services are also URI-addressable; for example, a URL to get a thumbnail of an image.

Some examples sites :

http://arrow.edu.au
http://www.lib.virginia.edu/digital/collections/
http://nsdl.org/
Dspace (http://www.dspace.org/)

DSPACE BASED DIGITAL LIBRARY

DSpace is open source software for building and managing Digital repositories. Developed jointly by MIT

Libraries and Hewlett-Packard (HP), is freely available to research institutions as an open source system that can be customized and extended. DSpace is a digital institutional repository that captures, stores, indexes, preserves, and redistributes content in digital formats Institutional Repository is a set of services that a research institution/ organization/ university offers to the members of its community for the management and dissemination of digital materials created by the institution and its community members Typically, DSpace has been deployed for Institutional Repositories of publications, thesis and dissertations. There are several groups working on extending its capabilities such implementation of ontology's in search interface and for submission module, customization for management of electronic theses and dissertations and for localization and international of the package for the world languages.

DSpace is designed for ease-of-use, with a web-based user interface that can be customized. The DSpace system provides a way to manage research materials and publications in a professionally maintained repository to give them greater visibility and accessibility over time.

WHY DSPACE WAS OPTED?

DSpace is an open source system with a robust database support for trouble free DL operations. The choice of the software for a digital library should be based upon the nature of collections, data formats, applications, user expectations and infrastructure. Institutional repositories mostly comprise of resources such as publications, theses and dissertations and presentations. Ideally, for such collections the system should have simple installation, configuration and management facilities. This is especially required as in many instances collection building and its management maybe decentralized. Dspace has the following features that have made it popular choice for building DLs:

- Dspace is an open source technology platform which can be customized and its

  - Capabilities can be extended
  - Dspace is a service model for open access and/ or digital archiving for perpetual access.
- Dspace is a platform to build an Institutional Repository* and the collections are searchable and retrievable by the Web. To make available institution-based scholarly material in digital formats. The collections will be open and interoperable.

WORKING WITH DSPACE

After installation and configuration all other functions such as building the collection, its organization, submission, review process, access and retrieval can be managed at distributed locations over the networks. The administrator is firstly responsible for implementing the information model and organizing the DL into communities and collections. The administrator can also delegate certain administrative tasks to others. Further tasks such as reviewing metadata verification is assigned to members. The admin creates groups of users (for instance grouping according to the departments they belong to) and authenticates users who can submit to the collection. Users can register themselves as members. Members can subscribe to entire collections or sub-collections depending on their interests. Mail alerts are sent to the members of each collection whenever a resource is added to that collection. Members authenticated by admin as 'submitters' can submit resources to the collection. The submitters are required to furnish metadata, basically Dublin Core data, for the resource they are submitting to the DL. Resources with a multiple files (such as website) can also be submitted. The submitters are required to agree with the terms and condition of licensing set forth by the DL before their submission can be passed on for review process. License information for every resource is stored. Dspace supports many popular data formats and has the provision for registering new bit stream formats.

Dspace is compliant with OAI-PMH version 2.0 and metadata in Dspace digital libraries can be harvested. Further there are various ways of access permissions that can be given to the items in the collections thereby even highly classified information can be part of the collection but be made visible to only the person who may be authenticated by policies to view them.

ARCHITECTURE AND SYSTEM REQUIREMENTS

- The DSpace system is organized into three layers, each of which consists of a number of components.
- The storage layer: responsible for physical storage of metadata and content.
- The business logic layer: deals with managing the content of the archive, users of the archive (e-people), authorization, and workflow.
- The application layer: containing components that communicate with the networked world outside of the individual DSpace installation, for example, the Web user interface and the modules for metadata harvesting service.

It is not enough to just use open source software, as they are free. It is equally important to examine whether the technologies needed to support it are also open and based on open standards. DSpace was developed to be open source, and in such a way that institutions and organizations with minimal resources could use it. The system is designed to run on the UNIX platform, and comprises other open source middleware and tools, and programs written by the DSpace team. All original code is in the Java programming language. Other pieces of the technology stack include a relational database management system (PostgreSQL), a Web server (Apache) and Java servlet engine (Tomcat), Jena (an RDF toolkit from HP Labs), OAICat from OCLC, and several other useful libraries. All these leveraged components and libraries are also open source software. The system is available on Source Forge (www.sourceforget.net), linked from both the DSpace informational web site and the HP Labs site (2).

INFORMATION MODEL AND COLLECTION ORGANIZATION

Generally DL collections are categorized according to institutional structure and functions. Before any implementation of the Dl software the DL library managers have to make a clear plan of the collection structure as suited for the purpose of the organization. DSpace has a well-planned information model to implement the collection structure. The digital library is divided into communities at the highest level. The communities can correspond to the different departments and units of an institution or organization. Communities further may have sub-communities within them. As of DSpace version 1.2, these communities can be organized into a hierarchy. Communities contain collections, which in turn contain items. Items are the actual resources that are uploaded into the DLs. Each item may belong to one collection. Each item contains bitstreams that are the computer files that make up the DL resource.

DSPACE SEARCH SYSTEM

The end user can browse, search and access the collections using the hierarchies and also the alphabetic bar menu. For searching the collection, Dspace uses Lucene Search Engine, which is a part of Apache Jakarta Project (1). Additionally research projects such as the ...(Portugal)... provides Ontologies that enables context-based querying. This work like subject based directory structures. Lucene search engine has very powerful search features that encompass many search approaches of the end-user. It provides the basic 'exact term' or keyword search. In addition, it allows fielded search akin the field level search of library databases. In Dspace, Dublin Core elements are used for the field names. Lucene also facilitates Boolean search, range searches, term boosting and proximity searches. The interesting search facility lucene uses fuzzy logic that is based on the Levenstien's alogorithm (5) that can replace and match terms by similarity. This feature is especially useful in instances where we hear a term and guess it spellings and more so in the case of personal names.

DATA FORMATS

Resources are stored as bit streams in Dspace repositories. In DSpace, a bit stream format is a unique and consistent way to refer to a particular file format. Each bit stream is associated with one Bit stream Format. Dspace supports most of the popular file formats. However, it adapts varied levels for different file types. Actually these are levels set by the host institution of the DL what data formats they may be able to support at what level. By and large, the three levels are categorized as:

- **Supported**: The format is recognized and the host institution will be responsible to make it usable in future also.
- **Known**: The format is recognized, and the hosting institution will promise to preserve the bit stream as-is, and allow it to be retrieved. The hosting institution will attempt to obtain enough information to enable the format to be upgraded to the 'supported' level.
- **Unsupported**: The format is unrecognized, but the hosting institution will undertake to preserve the bit stream as-is and allow it to be retrieved.

METADATA

DSpace users deal with/come across metadata in the following modules:

- Administration modules: Dublin core registry, administrative metadata—default values, mail alert to subscribers
- Submission modules: descriptive metadata
- Harvesting—OAI-PMH using the DC elements (unqualified)

- Search·result display: brief and full metadata. Metadata in DSpace is of three types:

Descriptive Metadata

Dublin core qualified set of elements is used. Each item has one Dublin Core metadata record. Basically Dublin core has about 15 elements and the total qualifies set brings it up to 65 elements.

Administrative Metadata

This includes preservation metadata, provenance and authorization policy data.

Structural Metadata

This includes information about how to present an item, or bit streams within an item, to an end-user, and the relationships between constituent parts of the item. Basically it is implementation of the Metadata Encoding and Transmission Standard (METS). It is partially implemented in Dspace up to the version 1.2.1

METADATA HARVESTING

Dspace is compliant with the OAI-PMH version 2.0 (7) for exposing metadata. OAI-PMH allows repositories to expose a hierarchy of sets in which records may be placed. DSpace exposes collections as sets. Each collection has a corresponding OAI·set and harvesters use a verb (OAI- command) List Sets, to discover the sets. Only the 15 basic Dublin Core elements is exposed at present.

PERSISTENT IDENTIFIERS

One of the common concerns of Digital library patrons is that online resources are volatile and may change or simply disappear. The idea of persistent identifiers of DLs is that it would be possible to find and retrieve deposited items in future and thus gain trust of the patrons. In particular, it is considered crucial that citations to archived material, whether found in printed articles or online, remain valid for long periods. DSpace has implemented CNRI handles (5) as the persistent identifier associated with each item. The CNRI Handle System covers assignment, management, and resolution of these persistent identifiers (or "handles").

Digital libraries today encompass a variety of resources, patrons and accordingly varied applications. The software package that powers DLs should therefore take into consideration the popular expectations of DLs. Dspace is designed for institutional repositories and is built with the MIT's experience of building institutional repositories. The features are quite adequate and useful for building institutional repositories. Further, it uses world standards and open standards for the DL operations that enhance its tenacity to bear with the technology upgrades in future.

India following institute using DSpace software:

- Bangalore Management Academy, Bangalore
- Indian Institute of Management, Kozhikode
- Indira Gandhi National Open University (IGNOU), New Delhi
- Institute of Petroleum Management, Gandhinagar
- IndiSarai Multimedia Digital Archive, Delhi
- Vidyanidhi Digital Library & amp; E-Scholarship Portal
- An Institute of Technology, Bombay, India
- Indian Statistical Institute, Library, Bangalor, Delhi College of Engineering, Delhi
- ETD of Indian Institute of Science, Bangalore
- Guru Gobind Singh Indraprastha University, New Delhi
- ICFAI Business School, Ahmedabad
- Indian Institute of Astrophysics, Bangalore

- Information And Library Network Centre (INFLIBNET), Ahmedabad
- Librarians' Digital Library (LDL) at DRTC, Bangalore
- M. N. Dastur & Company (P) Ltd, Kolkata
- National Chemical Laboratory, Pune
- National Institute of Oceanography (NIO), Goa
- National Institute of Technology, Rourkela
- Raman Research Institute, Bangalore

7

Computer Networks

The concept of the computer centre as a room with a large computer to which users bring their work for processing is totally obsolete now. The old model of a single computer serving all of the organizations computational needs has been replaced by one in which a large number of separate but interconnected do the job.

"Network is a processing complex consisting of two or more interconnected computers". Topology is the geometric configuration of devices on a network".

NETWORK TOPOLOGIES

Topology is the geometric arrangement of the computers in a network. Common topologies include :

- Star,
- Ring and
- Bus.

STAR NETWORK

The star network is frequently used to connect one or more small computers or peripheral devices to a large host computer or CPU. Many organizations use the star network or a variation of it in a time-sharing system, in which several users are able to share a central processor.

In a time-sharing setup, each terminal receives a fixed amount of the central CPU's time, called a time slice. Actually, because the CPU operates so much faster than terminals, one may not probably even notice that the CPU is away.

By establishing time-sharing, many people in a large organization can use a centralized computing facility. Time-sharing can also be purchased from an outside service, which is an economical way to operate for a small company that cannot afford its own large computer.

Star network is frequently used in a LAN to connect several microcomputers to a central unit that works as a communications controller. If the user of one microcomputer wants to send a document or message to a user at another computer, the message is routed through the central communications controller.

Another common use of the star network is as a LAN to connect several microcomputers to a mainframe computer that allows access to an organizations database.

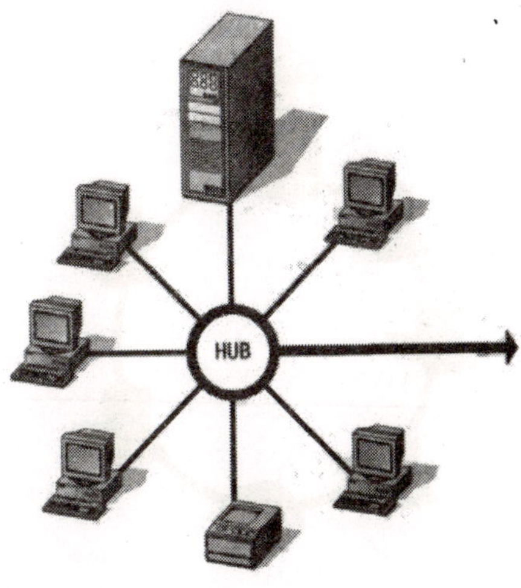

STAR TOPOLOGY

Access and control of star networks typically is maintained by a polling system. Polling means that the central computer or communications controller "polls" or asks each device in the network for it has a message to send and then allows each in turn to transmit data.

RING NETWORK

The ring network is a local-area network (LAN) whose topology is a ring. It can be as simple as a circle or point-to-point connections of computers at dispersed locations. There may not be a central host computer or communications controller. That is, all of the nodes are connected in a closed loop.

Messages travel around the ring, with each node reading those messages addressed to it. One of the advantages of ring networks is that they can span larger distances than other types of networks, such as bus networks, because each node regenerates messages as they pass through it.

Access and control of ring networks are typically maintained by a "token-passing" system. IBM's Token-Ring network is thought by observers to be a watershed event comparable to the development of the IBM PC itself.

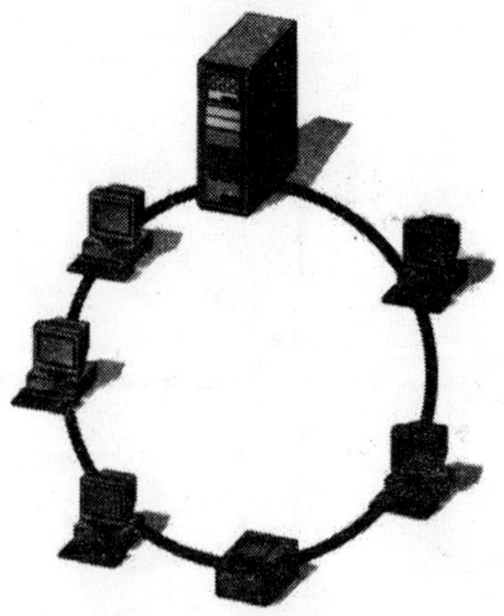

Token-Ring network is designed to link all types of computers together, including not only personal computers but also possibly minicomputers and mainframes. A Token-Ring network resembles a merry-go-round. To deliver a message, you would hand your addressed note to a rider (the token) on the merry-go-round, who would drop it off at the appropriate place.

BUS NETWORK

Bus networks are similar to ring networks except that the ends are not connected. All communications are carried on a common cable or bus and are available to each device on the network.

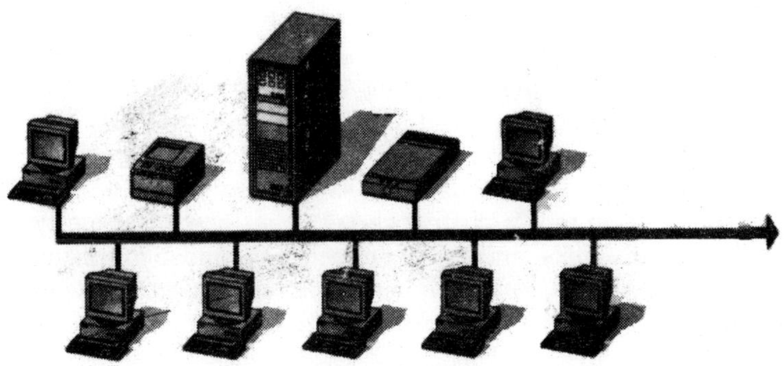

BUS TOPOLOGY

Access and control of bus networks are typically maintained by a method called contention, whereby if a line is unused, a terminal or device can transmit its message at will, but if two or more terminals initiate messages simultaneously, they must stop and transmit again at different intervals.

TYPES OF THE COMPUTER NETWORKS

There are three types of network

- LAN
- MAN
- WAN

LOCAL AREA NETWORKS (LAN)

LAN is a computer network that spans a relatively small area. Most lanes are confined to single building or group of buildings, however. One LAN can be connected to other LANs over any distance via telephone lines and radio waves. A system on LANs connected in this way is called a wide-area network (WAN).

[* File contains invalid data | In-line.JPG *]

Most LANs connect workstations and personal computers. Each node in a LAN has its own CPU with which it executes programs but it is also able to access data and device anywhere o the LAN, This means that many users can share expensive devices, such as laser printers, as well as data, users can also use the LAN to communicate with each other, by sending e-mail or engaging in chat sessions.

There are many different types of LANs-token-ring networks, Ethernets, and ARCnets being the most common for PCs. Most Apple Macintosh networks are based on Apples Apple talk network system, which is built in Macitosh computers.

LANs are capable of transmitting data at very fast rates much faster than data can be transmitted over a telephone line; but the distance are limited, and there is also a limit on the number if computers that can be attached to a single LAN.

METROPOLITAN AREA NETWORK (MAN)

A metropolitan area network (MAN) is a communications network covering a geographic area, the size of a city or suburb. A network that connects two or more LANs or CANs together but does not extend beyond the boundaries of the immediate town, city, or metropolitan area. Multiple routers, switches and hubs are connected to create a MAN. Attempts are being made to develop this type of network in metropolitan areas such Delhi, Calcutta, Bangalore, Madras, etc.

Broadly we can say that MAN is a data network designed for a town or city. In terms of geographic breadth, MANs are larger than local-area networks (LANs), but smaller than wide-area networks (WANs). MANs are usually characterized by very high-speed connections using fiber optical cable or other digital media. The purpose of a MAN is often to avoid long-distance telephone charges. Cellular phone systems are often MANs.

WIDE AREA NETWORK (WAN)

A WAN is a computer network that spans relatively large geographical areas. Typical a WAN consistent of two or more local area networks (LANs)

Computers connected to a wide area network are often connected through public networks, such as the telephone system, they can also be connected through lines or satellites, the largest WAN in existence in the Internet.

Computers connected to a wide-area network are often connected through public networks such as the telephone system. They can also be connected through leased lines or satellites. The largest WAN in existence is the Internet.

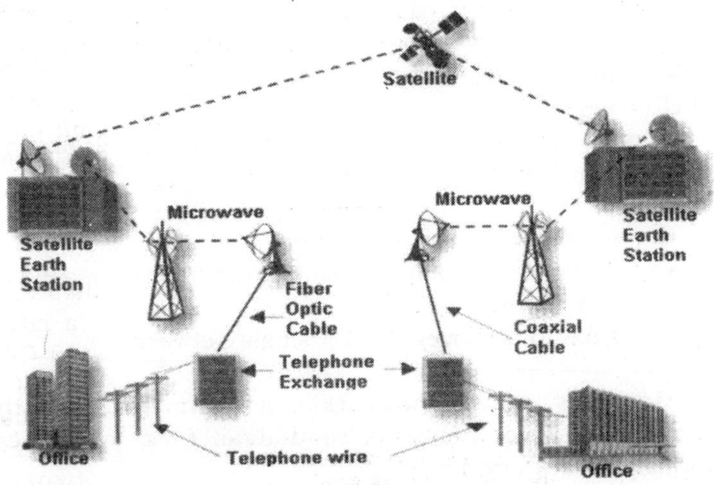

A TYPICAL WAN SETUP

Internet

Computers are in use for educational and informational purposes since many years. Internet, in the context of information storage, organization and retrieval, has become omnipotent. Today the number of Internet users doubles in every ten days. It shows the importance of the Internet and its usage. Internet has become a part of the structure of everyday life. It has changed the way of accessing information. Personal computers have come within the reach of the common man. Internet reduces time and distance and the globe into a small village.

INTERNET—CONCEPT

Internet is the world's largest computer network, the network of networks, scattered all over the world. It was created nearly 30 years ago as a project for the U.S. Department of Defense. Its goal was to create a method for widely separated computers to transfer data efficiently whether war or peace. From a handful of computer and users in the 1960s.

Today the Internet has grown to thousands of regional networks that connect millions of users round the earth. Any single individual, company, or country does not own this global network.

A network of networks, or Internet, is a group of networks that are:

- Interconnected physically
- Capable of communicating and sharing data with each other
- Able to act together as a single network.

Machines on one network can communicate with machines on other networks send data, files, and other information back and forth.

For this to work, the networks and machines that are part of the Internet have to agree either to speak the same "language" when they are communicating or to use an "interpreter." This "language" is known as software that enables the different types of machines on separate networks to communicate and exchange information.

To be used by different types of machines and yet be understood by all of them, the software must follow a set of rules. Those set of rules are called protocol. The Internet, with a capital "I," is the network of networks, which either uses the TCP/IP protocol or interacts with TCP/IP networks via gateways (the interpreters). The Internet presents these networks as one, seamless network for its users.

Internet covers the globe and includes large, international networks as well as many smaller, local-area networks (LANs).

Internet offers access to data, graphics, voice, sound, software, text, and people through a variety of services and tools for communication and data exchange. The value of Internet is highly commendable due to three obvious reasons.

Internet is the Cheapest and Fastest Means to

- Get information
- Provide information
- Compile information

Given below is a list of activities that one could do with a web browser:

- Visit websites
- Send and receive electronic mail
- Read and post articles in newsgroups
- Download files to your PC
- Chat with other users online
- Play games with others online
- Access on-line multimedia including radio and video broadcasts
- Search the Internet for information
- Join contests
- Contribute articles, and other materials

- Do online shopping and find jobs
- Post one's resume on the Internet
- Create your own websites
- Create an Email account
- Use the Email reminder service
- Find a person's details
- Send greetings to others.

The above list is by no means a complete and comprehensive one. There are a lot of other things that one can do on the Internet.

HISTORY OF INTERNET

"In 1957, the Soviet Union launched the first satellite, Sputnik I, triggering the US military to create the DARPA agency to regain the technological lead.

The IPTO (Information Processing Techniques Office) funded the research that led to the development of the ARPANET—Advanced Research Projects Agency".

"DARPA worked on developing technologies to protect the US against a space-based nuclear attack.

Some people in the IPTO considered the potential benefits of a country-wide communications network. Lawrence Roberts led development of the network architecture, and based it on the new idea of packet switching, first discovered by Leonard Kleinrock."

In October, 1969, the ARPANET first went live with communications between the University of California at Los Angeles and the Stanford Research Institute. The first networking protocol used on the ARPANET was the Network Control Program.

In 1983, it was replaced with the TCP/IP protocol developed by Bob Kahn and Vinton Cerf, which is still the standard used today.

In 1990, the National Science Foundation took over the management of what was then called the NSFNet, and significantly expanded its reach by connecting it to the CSNET in Universities throughout North America, and later to the EUnet throughout research facilities in Europe. In large part to the NSF's enlightened management, and fueled by the growing popularity of the web, the use of the net has been exploding.

INTERNET SERVICES

The World Wide Web allows access many distinct Internet services through a common set of protocols. A single application, the Web browser (e.g., Mozilla, Firefox, Internet Explorer, Lynx), can access most of these services and typically has the ability to launch helper applications. They can use plug-ins for services and file types it cannot access directly. The format of the Web address, or URL, indicates what kind of service the browser will access. Some of the more common formats include:

HTTP: The Hypertext Transfer Protocol is the protocol used to access most Web pages, images, and other file types on the World Wide Web.

HTTPS: Secure HTTP typically serves pages where financial or private information is to be entered, using Secure Sockets Layer (SSL).

FTP: File Transfer Protocol is used to move files between computers attached to the Internet.

Usenet: With the nntp://prefix, one can access Usenet newsgroups on specific news servers. In most cases, a Web browser will access a newsgroup from a news server specified in its settings.

Electronic mail: With the mail to prefix, the Web browser can send mail to a specific address, though one must first configure an SMTP server address to do so.

Telnet: Telnet is a protocol that emulates a terminal interface to remote hosts. Most Web browsers will launch a helper application for Telnet connections.

Local files: Though local files do not pertain to an Internet service, one can use a Web browser to view them and to navigate directories on a personal computer.

Gopher: A service that has been eclipsed by the World Wide Web, Gopher is a means of providing information online.

WAIS: WAIS stands for "Wide Area Information Servers". Web browsers rarely access WAIS directly. Rather, it is a directory service that CGI programs sometimes use.

STANDARDS

The Internet, a loosely-organized international collaboration of autonomous, interconnected networks, supports host-to-host communication through voluntary adherence to open protocols and procedures defined by Internet Standards. There are also many isolated interconnected networks, which are not connected to the global Internet but use the Internet Standards.

The Internet Standards Process is concerned with all protocols, procedures, and conventions that are used in or by the Internet, whether or not they are part of the TCP/IP protocol suite. In case of protocols developed and/or standardized by non-Internet organizations, however, the Internet Standards Process normally applies to the application of the protocol or procedure in the Internet context, not to the specification of the protocol itself.

In general, an Internet Standard is a specification that is stable and well-understood. It is technically competent, has multiple, independent, and interoperable implementations. It is recognizably useful in some or all parts of the Internet.

Internet is the works largest computer network, the network of networks, networks of networks, or "internet", is a group of two or more networks that are:

- Interconnected physically.
- Capable of communicating and sharing data with each other.
- Able to act together as a single network.

Machines on one network can communicate with machines on there networks, and send data, files, and other information back and forth. Internet covers the globe and include large international networks a well as many smaller, local-area networks. Internet offers access to data graphics, sound, software, text and people through a variety of services and tools for communicators and data exchange :

- ❖ Remote login (teletext)
- ❖ File transfers (FTP)
- ❖ Electronic mails (E-Mail)
- ❖ News (USENET)
- ❖ Hypertext (WWW)

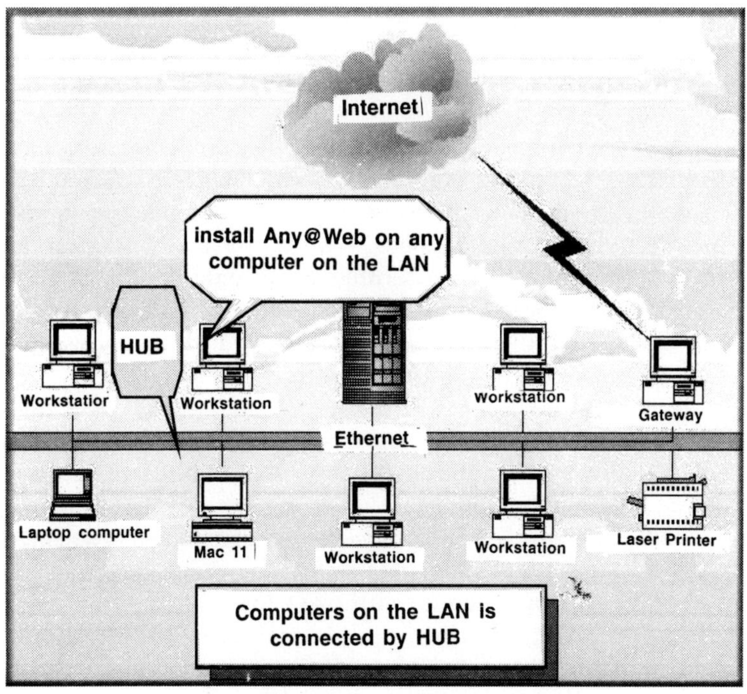

WHAT ARE SPECIALS ABOUT INTERNET?

There are three obvious reasons; Internet is the cheapest and fastest means to:

- Get information
- Provide information
- Compile information

GETTING INFORMATION ON THE INTERNET

The amount of information available through the Internet is staggering. To make all of it more easily available to users, programs such as the gopher were developed to help present material in some logical fashion, The most recent and very successful attempt at presenting information over the internet is the World Wide Web you could get information about people. Products, Organizations, research data electronic versions of the printed media etc from the Internet.

PROVIDING INFORMATION ON THE INTERNET

Most of what you want to provide could be considered advertising, while that may sound somewhat commercial, it is the best and most inexpensive way to let people know who you are, what you are doing, have done and how. For an organization or institution setting up a home page is a good way to let the world know what its products and services are. In addition to advertising, the other critical functions that relate to provision of information are.

- **Publishing,** include full text articles, reports illustrated articles, abstracts computer programs and demonstrations.
- **Extension**, in which some of the delays associated with the printed media, may be reduced.
- **Teaching**, the possibilities on her include both distance learning and assistant for students, Compiling information from the Internet.

There is obviously a special case of "getting" information. The distinction is that it is possible to get specialized information from the web. For instance if you wanted to poll the readership for a magazines or conduct a survey to detect the pulse of selected community, the web provides you with the ideal platform and opportunity. Using forms, e-mail, etc., you can conducts survey, get opinion of peoples across the world. There are hundreds of discussion groups and list servers, where one can post a question and get in answered by hindered of people who participate in these discussions.

INTERNET ACCESS

You can connect to the Internet in one of two basis ways, dialing into an Internet service Providers computer, or with a direct connection to an Internet services provider. The difference is mainly in the speed and cost.

In the most cases, you connect to ISP using telephone and modem.

DIAL-UP CONNECTION

With a dial-up account, you use your modern to convert computer bits and bytes into o modulated signals that the phone lines can transmit these signal are received by a modem at your ISP and demodulated into bits and bytes for their computer, "Modem" is short for "modulator-demodulate." You usually connect to a local ISP and can surf or browse the Internet. Dial-up access is either by way of serial line Internet Protocol.

DIRECT CONNECTION

We can also get a direct connection to your ISP, where you have a fixed cable or deducted phone line the ISP. Often the dedicated line is an ISDN (integrated services Digital Networks) line which is a higher-speed versions of the standard phone line, but actually requires two phone lines. ISDN can handle more than 56.600 bps. ISDN line scale upward, meaning you can transparently add more line to get faster speeds with single ISDN connections, up to about 1.28 million bps.

GENERAL SERVICE

Given below is a list of activities that you could do with a web browser:

- visit web sites
- Send and receive electronic mail
- Read and post articles in newsgroups
- Download files to your PC
- Chat with other users on-line
- Play games with others on-line
- Access on-line multimedia including radio and video broadcasts
- Search the Internet for information
- Subscribe to electronic newsletters, e-magazines, etc.
- Join contests
- Contribute articles, and other materials
- Do on-line shopping
- Post your resumes on the Internet
- Create your own web sites
- Create an e-mail remainder service
- Find a person's details
- Send flowers or gifts to others.

The above list is by no means a complete and comprehensive one. You can do many other things on the Internet.

INTERNET PROTOCOLS

We will examine the various Internet protocols used. The most commonly used protocols are:

- Transmission Control Protocol/Internet Protocol (TCP/IP)
- File Transfer Protocol (FTP)
- Hyper Text Transfer Protocol (HTTP)
- Telnet
- Gopher
- Wide Area Information Service (WAIS)

TRANSMISSION CONTROL PROTOCOL/INTERNET PROTOCOL (TCP/IP)

TCP/IP stands for Transmission Control Protocol/Internet

Protocol. TCP/IP IS Actually a collection of protocol, or rules, that govern the way data travels from one machine to another across networks. The Internet is based on TCP/IP. TCP/IP has two major components: TCP and IP.

IP : The IP component does the following:

- Envelopes and addresses the data.
- Enables the network to read the envelope and forward the data to its destination.
- Defines how much data can fit in a single" envelope" (a packet).

The relationship between data, IP, and networks is often compared to the relationship between a letter, its addressed envelope, and the postal system. The addressed and packaged data is sent over the network to its destination.

TCP : The TCP component does the following:

- Breaks data up into packers that the network can handle efficiently.
- Verifies whether all the packets have arrived at their destination.
- "Reassembles" the data.

TCP/IP can be compared to moving across country. You pack your house in boxes and put your new address on them. The moving company picks them up; makes a list of the boxes, and ships them across country along the most efficient route – this may mean putting your dishes and your bedroom furniture on different trucks, your belongings arrive at your new address. You consult your list to make sure that everything you shipped has arrived (in good shape), and then you unpack your boxes and "reassemble" your house.

FILE TRANSFER PROTOCOL (FTP)

FTP stands for File Transfer Protocol, and is part of the TCP/IP protocol suite. It is the protocol, or set of rules, which enables files to be transferred between computers. RTP is a powerful tool which allows files to be transferred from "computer A" to "computer B", or *vice versa*.

FTP works on the client/server principle. A client program enables the user to interact with server in order to access information and services on the server access these files, an RTP client program is used. This interface allows the user to locate the file to be transferred and initiate the transfer process.

The Basic Steps to use FTP

1. Connect to the FTP server.
2. Navigate the file structure to find the file you want.
3. Transfer the file.

The specifics of each step will vary, depending on the client program being used and the type of Internet connection. Anonymous RTP allows a user to access or password is needed.

However, an anonymous FTP site will sometimes ask that users login with the name "anonymous" and use their electronic mail address as the password.

There are wide varieties of files that are publicly available through anonymous FTP :

Shoftware—software that you can use free for a trial period but then pay a fee for.

Freeware—completely free software, for example fonts, clipart and games.

Upgrades & Patches—upgrades to current software and "fixes" for software problems.

Documents—examples include research papers, articles and Internet documentation.

Files on FTP servers are often compressed. Compression decreases file size. This enables more files to be stored on the server and makes file transfer times shorter. In order to use a compressed file to be stored on the server and makes file transfer times shorter. In order to use a compressed file it needs to be decompressed using appropriate software. It is a good idea to have current virus checking software on the computer before files are transferred to it.

HYPERTEXT TRANSFER PROTOCOL (HTTP)

0HTTP is short for Hypertext Transfer Protocol. It is the set of rules, or protocol that governs the transfer of hypertext between two or more computers. The World Wide Web encompasses the universe of information that is available via HTTP.

Hypertext is text that is specially coded using a standard system called Hypertext Markup Language (HTML). The HTML codes are used to create links. These links can be textual or graphic, and when clicked on, can "link" the user to another resource such as other HTML documents, text files, graphics, animation and sound.

HTTP is based on the client/server principle. HTTP allows "computer A" (the client) to establish a connection with "computer B" (the server) and make a request. The server accepts the connection initiated by the client and sends back a response. An HTTP request identifies the resource that the client is interested in and tells the server what "action" to take on the resource.

When a user selects a hypertext link, the client program on their computer uses HTTP to contact the server, identify a resource, and ask the server to respond with an action. The server accepts the request, and then uses HTTP to respond to or perform the action.

Usually hypertext links will be blue in colors and will be underlined (this is the normal convention, which is not always followed). When you move the mouse pointer over a hypertext link the pointer changes its shape to that of a hand. In the case of text-based browsers, the hypertext links will be highlighted and you can navigate between them using the keyboard.

HTTP also provides access to other Internet protocols like File Transfer Protocol (FTP), Simple Mail Transfer Protocol (SMTP), Network News Transfer Protocol (NNTP).

TELNET

Telnet is a protocol, or set of rules, that enables one computer to connect to another computer. This process is also referred to as remote login.

The user's computer, which initiates the connection, is referred to as the local computer, and the machine being connected to, which accepts the connection, is referred to as the remote, or host commuter. The remote computer can be physically located in the next room, the next town, or in another country.

Once connected, the user's computer emulates the remote computer. When the user types in commands, they are executed on the remote computer. The user's monitor displays what is taking place on the remote computer during the telnet session.

The procedure for connecting to a remote computer will depend on how your Internet access is set-up. Once a connection to a remote computer is made, instructions or menus may appear. Some remote machines may require a user to have an account on the machine, and may prompt users for a username and password. Many resources, such as library catalogs, are available via telnet without an account and password.

Telnet also operates on the client/server principle. The local computer uses a telnet client program to establish the connection and display data on the local computer's monitor. The remote, or host, computer uses a telnet server program to accept the connection and send responses to requests for information back to the local computer.

Telnet allows the user to access Internet resources on other computers around the world. A variety of resources is available through telnet. For example, Library catalogs, Databases, other Internet tools such as FTP, Gopher, and the World Wide Web, etc.

GOPHER

Gopher is a protocol designed to search retrieve and display documents from remote sites on the Internet. In addition to document display, document retrieval, it is possible to initiate on-line connections with other systems via Gopher. It accomplishes this using the client/server model of users running "client" software on their local machines that provide an interface that interacts with remote "servers" or computers that have information of interest.

Information accessible via Gopher is stored on many computers all over the Internet. These computers are called Gopher servers. Information stored on many kinds of non-gopher servers is also available via special Gopher servers that act as gateways (protocol translators). Virtually any popular computer (Mac, UNIX box, PC, or larger computer) can be used as a server. Servers do not just contain files, directories and searchable databases; they can also contain references to other servers. To retrieve and search this information, you need to run a Gopher client application on your computer. Turbo Gopher is a Gopher client application.

Users interact with Gopher via a hierarchy of menus and can use full-text searching capabilities of Gopher to identify desired documents. Once an appropriate item is selected, Gopher retrieves it from wherever on the network it resides and (if it is text) displays it. The user may feel as if all the information available to Gopher resides on their local computer, when in fact Gopher is interacting with a large number of independently owned and operated computers around the world. Gopher client software exists for most computer platforms.

Gopher was created as a piece of software to utilize some of the services that was becoming available on the Internet. It was designed to work with a variety of different Internet stand-alone services. The integration of many services into Gopher has made the Internet an easier medium to navigate.

Gopher can work with the following Internet tools or systems

- Search local WAIS indices; query remote WAIS servers and funnel the results to Gopher clients.
- Query remote FTP sites and funnel the results to Gopher clients.

- Be queried bowwow clients either using built in Gopher querying or using native HTTP querying.

WAIS

WAIS (pronounced "ways") stands for Wide Area Information Service. WAIS is an Internet search tool that is based on the Z39.50 standard. The Z39.50 standard describes a protocol, or set of rules, for computer-to-computer information retrieval.

WAIS also works on the client/server principle. A WAIS client program enables the user's computer to contact a WAIS server, submit a search query, and receive a response to that query.

INTERNET ADDRESSING

In general, Internet addressing is a systematic way to identify people, commuters and internet resources. On the Internet, the term "address" is used loosely. Address can mean many different things from an electronic mail address to a URI.

IP ADDRESS

If you want to connect to another computer, transfer files to or from another computer, or send an e-mail message, you first need to know where the other computer is-you need the computer address.

An IP (Internet Protocol) address is an identifier for a particular machine on particular network; it is part of a scheme to identify computers on the Internet. IP addresses are also referred to as IP numbers and Internet addresses. An IP address consists of four sections separated by periods. Each section contains a number ranging from 0 to 225. Example; 202.45, 1.6. These four sections represent both the machine itself, or hostm, and the network that the host is on. The network portion of the IP address is allocated to Internet Service Providers (ISPs) by the InterNIC, under authority of the Internet Assigned Numbers Authority (IANA). ISPs then assign the host portion of the IP address to the machines on the networks that they operate.

THE IP ADDRESSES HAVE THE FOLLOWING CHARACTERISTICS IN COMMON:

- IP addresses are unique,
- No two machines can have the same IP number.
- IP addresses are also global and standardized.
- All machines connected to the Internet agree to use the same scheme for establishing an address.

UNIFORM RESOURCE LOCATOR (URL)

A URL identifies a particular Internet resource; for example a Web page, a Gopher server, a library catalog, an image, or a text file, URLs represent a standardized addressing scheme for Internet resources, and help the users to locate these resources by indicating exactly where they are. Every resource available via the World Wide Web has a unique URL.

URLs consist of letters, numbers, and punctuation. The basic structure of a URL Is hierarchical, and the hierarchy moves from left to right:

Examples

1. http://www.Inl.net/alexis/index.html
2. gopher://gopher. State.edu/
3. ftp://ftp.xyz.com/

WEB BROWSERS

A browser is a piece of software that acts as an interface between the user and the inner-workings of the Internet, specifically the World Wide Web Browsers are also referred to as web clients, or Universal Clients, because in the client/ server model, the browser functions as the client program.

The browser acts on behalf of the use. The browser:

- Contacts a web server and sends a request for information.
- Receives the information and then displays it on the user's computer.

A browser can be graphical or text-based and can make the Internet easier to use and more intuitive. A text-based browser shows the user only the textual matter. A graphical photographs and multimedia.

Examples of some common browsers are:

- Netscape Navigator
- Microsoft Internet Explorer
- Mosaic
- Opera
- Amaya
- Hot Java
- Lynx (Text-based).

WEB BROWSING

Internet browsing or "net surfing", as it is often called, is the process of visiting different web sites on the Internet hosted by various companies, organizations, educational institutions, magazines, individuals, etc. The Internet contains a wealth of information that can help your business. Armed with a good Internet browser, you can easily get around to the myriad of sites, gathering competitive information, conducting market research, reading publications, and staying in touch with what's happening at your business associations.

SEARCHING THE WEB

The World Wide Web has emerged as a viable and legitimate way to publish information. Experience is starting to suggest that certain kind of information can be found more effectively on the web than it can be found using print sources. Until recently, surfing was a typical approach for finding information on the web. Surfing is instructed and options browsing, starting with a particular web page, the approach is to follow links from page to page make educated guesses along the way, hoping sooner or later to arrive at the desired piece of information. Surfing is browsing with out tool.

There are two main types of search tools: web index and search engines.

WEB INDEX

A web index is designed to assist user in locating information on the World Wide Web. Web index are also referred to as catalogs or directories, a web indexes collects and organizes resources available via the World Wide Web. There are a number of web index available.

The method of organization, as well as other features, many vary from one index to another. Some indexes may present information alphabetically; other may take a topical approach. Topical indexes often present their resources in a hierarchical arrangement, moving from general to more specific.

SEARCH ENGINES

Examples : http://www.yahoo.com
http://www.lycos.com

A web search engine is an interactive tool to help people locate information available via the World Wide Web. Web search engine are actually databases a contain reference to thousand of resource. User interacts with the database, submitting question that "ask" the database if it contains resource that match a specific criteria.

There are many search engines available on the web. A web search engine provides an interface between the user and the understanding database. The interface presents the user with a place to type in a search string, with may be a word, a phrase, a date, or some other criterion, and a way to submit the request.

The web search engine runs the search string against the database, returns a list of resource that matches the cineraria, and displays the results for the user. Many web search engines use "fill-out" forms as an interface, and support complex queries. Many also include instruction and tips to search the database more effectively. Because web search engine can use hypertext, user is able to link directly to resources listed in the display.

Some popular search engines
http://www.yahoo.com
http://www.google.com

META-SEARCH ENGINES

A web Meta-searcher is a tool that helps users locates information available via the World Wide Web. Web meta-searcher provides a single interface that enables users to search many different search engines, index, and databases simultaneously. There is a number of web meta-searcher available.

Because the content of search engine, index and database will vary, the same query typed into several search engines is likely to produce different results, when searching a topic, user often want to see results from various source. Meta search engines and indexes provide a collection, or databases of resource that can be queried.

- Single search engines and index provide a collection or databases of resource that can be queried.
- Meta-searchers do not provide databases. They provide a service that sends single query to multiple databases.

Example

http://www.search.com

INTERNET CHAT

Internet chat lets you communicate with people from all over the world, in real-time. There are many ways to chat with other internet user. you can use a large number of sites on the web you can use the customized chat facilities of the on-line service provider, or you can connect to telnet services devoted to chat. You can also use client software to access one of the network that host internet relay chat.

INTRANET

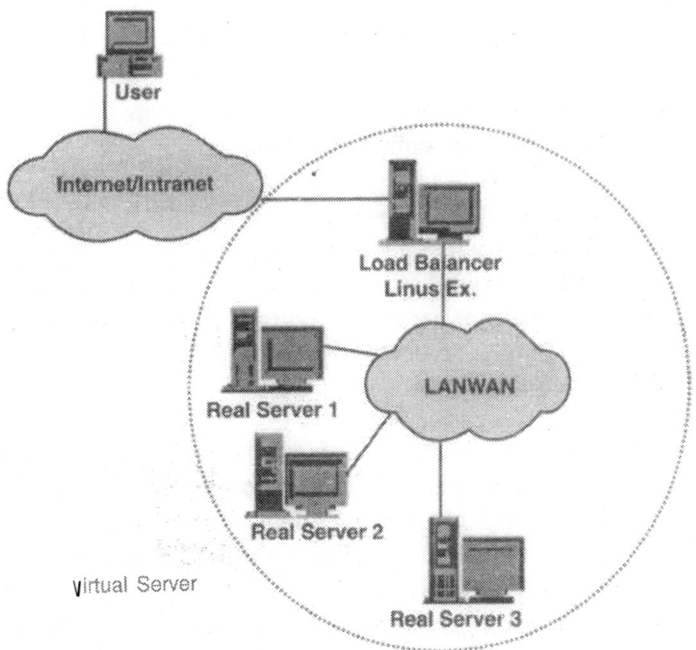

Intranet is a communication net work, which bridge the entire small computer networks world wide as a whole. Internet is abased upon Internet technology, in particular World Wide Web to build information system within organization. Internet connect people and organization and information source by using common protocols to link computer on a public and open-to-all basics, an intranet user the same common protocol for internal company or group purposes. Instead of adopting a common proprietary standard for its communications, information storage and presentation, etc., the company or institution decides to use internet standard and methods. An internet can be defined as a network connecting an affiliated set of client using standard internet protocol, esp. TCP/IP and HTTP or as an IP-based network nodes behind a firewall or behind several firewall connected by secure, possibly virtual network.

Characteristics of Intranet

Intranet inherits all the merits of Internet:

- **Openness**: Open architecture based on Internet.
- **Ease of use**: World Wide Web facilities it.
- **Low cost**: Low network cost, license free, client program install expense.
- **Flexibility**: easy to scale up and down.
- **Scalability**: Easy to scale up and down.
- **Innovation**: Easy to accommodation new technology.

Advantages of Intranet

- Compared with Client/Server architecture, it costs much less to build initial systems, which results in maximum efficiency and flexibility.
- It is based on Internet protocol, which expands accessibility worldwide.
- Consistent graphical user interface of web browser eliminates separate tutorial session.
- It handles multimedia data effortlessly.
- HTML, document facilities higher level of document exchanging scheme.
- Ready to access the information worldwide.
- Institute graphical user interface for every average skilled user.
- Fully support open standard and architecture for flexible expandability.
- Low administration and maintenances cost.
- Platform-independent system configuration features.

SEMANTIC WEB

The Semantic Web is an evolving extension of the World Wide Web in which the semantics of information and services on the web is defined, making it possible for the web to understand and satisfy the requests of people and machines to use the web content. It derives from World Wide Web Consortium director Sir Tim Berners-Lee's vision of the Web as a universal medium for data, information, and knowledge exchange.

At its core, the semantic web comprises a set of design principles, collaborative working groups, and a variety of enabling technologies. Some elements of the semantic web are expressed as prospective future possibilities that are yet to be implemented or realized. Other elements of the semantic web are expressed in formal specifications. Some of these include Resource Description Framework (RDF), a variety of data interchange formats (e.g. RDF/XML, N3, Turtle, N-Triples), and notations such as RDF Schema (RDFS) and the Web Ontology Language (OWL), all of which are intended to provide a formal description of concepts, terms, and relationships within a given knowledge domain.

BLOGS

The word "blog" is slang for web log. It refers to a regularly maintained journal or diary posted on the Internet. Within just a few years, the word went from invention to well known term around the world. This is a reflection of the awesome communication power of the World Wide Web. The word "blog" can be used as a noun to refer to the web log itself. It is also a verb denoting the act of contributing to a blog.

A frequent, chronological publication of personal thoughts and Web links.

This is popular Library science Blog

https://www.blogger.com/start

http://lislibraryblogger.blogspot.com/

Librarian.net

www.librarian.net

Librarian's Rant

WWW.lblog.jalcorn.net

LISNews

www.lisnews.com

The Shifted Librarian

www.theshiftedlibrarian.com

Travelin' Librarian

www.travelinlibrarian.blogspot.com

Information

A blog is often a mixture of what is happening in a person's life and what is happening on the Web, a kind of hybrid diary/guide site, although there are as many unique types of blogs as there are people.

People maintained blogs long before the term was coined, but the trend gained momentum with the introduction of automated published systems, most notably Blogger at blogger.com. Thousands of people use services such as Blogger to simplify and accelerate the publishing process.

Blogs are alternatively called web logs or weblogs. However, "blog" seems less likely to cause confusion, as "web log" can also mean a server's log files.

CONTENT MANAGEMENT SYSTEMS

A content management system (CMS) is a computer application used to create, edit, manage, and publish content in a consistently organized fashion. CMS are frequently used for storing, controlling, versioning, and publishing industry-specific documentation such as news articles, operators' manuals, technical manuals, sales guides, and marketing brochures. The content managed may include computer files, image media, audio files, video files, electronic documents, and Web content.

A CMS May Support the following features:

- Identification of all key users and their content management roles;
- the ability to assign roles and responsibilities to different content categories or types;
- definition of workflow tasks for collaborative creation, often coupled with event messaging so that content managers are alerted to changes in content (For example, a content creator submits a story, which is published only after the copy editor revises it and the editor-in-chief approves it);
- the ability to track and manage multiple versions of a single instance of content;
- the ability to capture content (e.g. scanning);
- (Increasingly, the repository is an inherent part of the system, and incorporates enterprise search and retrieval.);
- separation of content's semantic layer from its layout (For example, the CMS may automatically set the color, fonts, or emphasis of text.).

Web Content Management Systems

A web content management system is a CMS designed to simplify the publication of Web content to Web sites, in particular allowing content creators to submit content without requiring technical knowledge of HTML or the uploading of files.

http://www.library.iitb.ac.in/

Mumbai IIT using Joomla Software and Developing Library portal see the above URL.

RSS FEEDS

RSS is a family of Web feed formats used to publish frequently updated works—such as blog entries, news headlines, audio, and video—in a standardized format. An RSS document (which is called a "feed", "web feed", or "channel") includes full or summarized text, plus metadata such as publishing dates and authorship. Web feeds benefit publishers by letting them syndicate content quickly and automatically. They benefit readers who want to subscribe to timely updates from favored websites or to aggregate feeds from many sites into one place. RSS feeds can be read using software called an "RSS reader", "feed reader", or "aggregator", which can be web-based or desktop-based. A standardized XML file format allows the information to be published once and viewed by many different programs. The user subscribes to a feed by entering the feed's URI into the reader or by clicking an RSS icon in a browser that initiates the subscription process. The RSS reader checks the user's subscribed feeds regularly for new work, downloads any updates that it finds, and provides a user interface to monitor and read the feeds.

The initials "RSS" are used to refer to the following formats: "Really Simple Syndication (RSS 2.0)", "RDF Site Summary (RSS 1.0 and RSS 0.90)", or "Rich Site Summary (RSS 0.91)".

RSS formats are specified using XML, a generic specification for the creation of data formats. Although RSS formats have evolved since March 1999, the RSS icon ("") first gained.

http://rssfeedreader.com/

DEEP WEB OR INVISIBLE WEB

The *deep Web* (also called *Deepnet*, the *invisible Web*, or the *hidden Web*) refers to World Wide Web content that is not part of the surface Web, which is indexed by search engines. It is estimated that the deep Web is several orders of magnitude larger than the surface Web. Michael Bergman mentioned that Jill Ellsworth used the term "invisible Web" in 1994 to refer to websites that are not registered with any search engine. Bergman cited a January 1996 article by Frank Garcia: "It would be a site that's possibly reasonably designed, but they didn't bother to register it with any of the search engines. So, no one can find them! You're hidden. I call that the invisible Web."

Another early use of the term *invisible Web* was by Bruce Mount (Director of Product Development) and Matthew B. Koll (CEO/Founder) of Personal Library Software, Inc. (PLS) when describing the @1 deep Web tool. The term was used in a December 1996 press release from PLS.

DEEP RESOURCES

Deep Web resources may be classified into one or more of the following categories :

- Dynamic content—dynamic pages which are returned in response to a submitted query or accessed only through a form, especially if open-domain input elements (such as text fields) are used; such fields are hard to navigate without domain knowledge.
- Unlinked content—pages which are not linked to by other pages, which may prevent Web crawling programs from accessing the content. This content is referred to as pages without backlinks (or inlinks).
- Private Web—sites that require registration and login (password-protected resources).
- Contextual Web—pages with content varying for different access contexts (e.g., ranges of client IP addresses or previous navigation sequence).
- Limited access content—sites that limit access to their pages in a technical way (e.g., using the Robots Exclusion Standard, CAPTCHAs or pragma:no-cache/cache-control:no-cache [header]s), prohibiting search engines from browsing them and creating cached copies.
- Scripted content—pages that are only accessible through links produced by JavaScript as well as content dynamically downloaded from Web servers via Flash or AJAX solutions.

- Non-HTML/text content—textual content encoded in multimedia (image or video) files or specific file formats not handled by search engines.
http://deepwebresearch.blogspot.com/
http://lii.org/

Accessing

To discover content on the Web, search engines use web crawlers that follow hyperlinks. This technique is ideal for discovering resources on the surface Web but is often ineffective at finding deep Web resources. For example, these crawlers do not attempt to find dynamic pages that are the result of database queries due to the infinite number of queries that are possible. It has been noted that this can be (partially) overcome by providing links to query results, but this could unintentionally inflate the popularity (e.g., PageRank) for a member of the deep Web.

One way to access the deep Web is via federated search based search engines. Search tools such as Science.gov are being designed to retrieve information from the deep Web. These tools identify and interact with searchable databases, aiming to provide access to deep Web content.

EVALUATION OF WEB DOCUMENTS HOW TO INTERPRET THE BASICS

Accuracy of Web Documents :

Who wrote the page and can you contact him or her?

What is the purpose of the document and why was it produced?

Is this person qualified to write this document?

Accuracy

- Make sure author provides e-mail or a contact address/phone number.
- Know the distinction between author and Webmaster.

Authority of Web Documents :

Who published the document and is it separate from the "Webmaster?"

Check the domain of the document, what institution publishes this document?

Does the publisher list his or her qualifications?

Authority

- What credentials are listed for the authors)?
- Where is the document published? Check URL domain.

Objectivity of Web Documents :

What goals/objectives does this page meet?
How detailed is the information?
What opinions (if any) are expressed by the author?

Objectivity

- Determine if page is a mask for advertising; if so information might be biased.
- View any Web page as you would an infomercials on television. Ask yourself why was this written and for whom?

Currency of Web Documents :

When was it produced?
When was it updated?
How up-to-date are the links (if any)?

Currency

- How many dead links are on the page?
- Are the links current or updated regularly?
- Is the information on the page outdated?

Coverage of the Web Documents :

Are the links (if any) evaluated and do they complement the documents' theme?

Is it all images or a balance of text and images?

Is the information presented cited correctly?

Coverage

- If page requires special software to view the information, how much are you missing if you don't have the software?
- Is it free or is there a fee, to obtain the information?
- Is there an option for text only, or frames, or a suggested browser for better viewing?

WEB 2.0

In simple words, application of Web 2.0 in libraries is known as Library 2.0 or L2. Therefore, it is important to have a discussion on Web 2.0 at first before moving further. During the year 2000, when web under 'dot com' was getting crumbled up with the concept and general consideration that web is for publishing only. Even in this situation O'Reilly Media Inc. under the leadership of its founder Tim O'Reilly came out as strong believer of web. This group has highlighted the web as dynamic platform for productive communication, especially in the area of business and marketing. Originally Web 2.0 is a term originally coined by Dale Daugherty and Tim O'Reily in the year 2004 during a brainstorming session of a special conference organized to discuss the future of web and emerging techniques.

Web 2.0 is being defined differently by the experts, few say it is a technology which provides lively experience to the users while using the Internet and few say it is an advance stage of Internet. Other say it is optimum use of technologies over the Internet and few considered it as propaganda for Internet marketing. Though, web 2.0 is a user-centred web, where blogs, wikis, social networks, multimedia applications, dynamic programming scripts are being used for collection, contribution and collaboration concepts on the web.

LIBRARY 2.0

The term Library 2.0 is coined by Michael Casey in 2006. Various library professionals have defined the term differently but in general we can say that application of web 2.0 in libraries is known as Library 2.0. Now question arises how libraries have come into Web 2.0 business and this question is being discussed in many professional platforms. To answer this question, Five Laws of Library Science given by Dr. S.R. Ranganathan about a century ago are absolutely valid to justify transformation of libraries into Library 2.0. The laws are:

1. Information is for use (Books are for use).
2. Every user his/her information (Every reader his/ her book).
3. Every information its user (Every book its reader).
4. Save the time of the user (Save time of the reader).
5. The library is a growing organism (The library is a growing organism).

These laws are strictly showing users as centric force of any library system. First law recommends proper use of information. Second and third laws address right information to the right user and also about alert services. Forth law is asking to use new tools and technologies so librarians can save the time of user as well as library staff. Fifth law shows the broad spectrum of library system which is infinitive in nature and also recommending use of latest technologies, tools, services and methods as required to give vibrant and dynamic shape to the library system.

WEB 2.0 IN THE LIBRARIES

Library website: Library 2.0 is offering dynamic websites for the libraries, which embedded with semantic web and interoperability of various tools and techniques. Few of them are as:

- **Streaming media:** Streaming technology takes care of multimedia files over the Internet. It is the streaming of video and audio media that incorporate more interactive, media-rich facets. With the help of streaming media users can interact with library staff or their teachers as they interact in classrooms or instruction labs.
- **Mashups:** Mashup is a hybrid application of the web, which integrates information from different sources at one platform. In simple words it is an application that combines data or functionality from two or more external sources to create a new service. Mashup is the technology, which integrates all applications of web 2.0 at single platform.
- **Podcast:** Padcast defined as "a digital media file or collection of files that is distributed over the Internet periodically and made available for download by means of web syndication". The files can be played back on a computer or personal player, i.e. Ipod or mobile, etc.

OPAC

- **Tagging:** This makes information searching easier on the Internet. In which users can create and change the metadata, especially subject headings to the contents. This acts like an open catalogue to the information. In this users can give subject headings to their interested documents/contents and also write reviews of the contents. In web OPAC system users can tag their interested documents and also write comments and reviews on interested documents.

ALERT SERVICES

- **Instant Messaging:** In simple words it is known as "Chat", through this chat reference library users can interact with librarians on library related issues as they would interacting face to face. Instant messaging reference service is being used successfully and expertly in libraries.

- **Social Networks:** Social networking is the most promising and most talked technology of present days. This allows people to create virtual communities (personal or professional) over the Internet for interaction. Social Networks are online communities where people meet, socialize, exchange digital files, etc. Facebook, MySpace, Orkut and Flickr are few popular examples of Social Networks. Libraries can also start their social network about latest books or documents in the libraries where users can discuss or comments on the contents being contained by these books or documents. This can not be only restricted to books or other documents even library services and activities can also be discussed through this.
http://en.wikipedia.org/wiki/List_of_social_networking_websites

PUBLISHING

Blog: Jorn Barger coined 'Blog' in the year 1997 and blogs are being considered as a great milestone in the history of web publishing. This is a sort of personal web site featuring diary-type commentary, simple web posts and links to articles or other web sites. This is being frequently updated and gives chronological arrangement of the posts. For easy search each entry or post can be tagged with keyword and description. Libraries can start their blogs to encourage interactions amongst users and library staff. Blog can also be used for promoting activities and services of the libraries. It allows two ways interaction where users can also make comment on the posted information.

- **Wikis:** This is like an open web page and who have access permission can publish or edit the information on these wabpages by using their browsers. Professional communities are using wikis as reference guides that reflect the collective knowledge of the community. Wikipedia is the excellent example of this service. Libraries can open their webpages in the wikis and can promote social interaction among librarians and library users.

NOTICES

- **RSS Feeds:** RSS (Really Simple Syndication) is the technology, which facilitates users to keep track of new updates on selected websites. This technology normally is being seen in blogs and wikis but now almost all the websites are using this technology. To facilitate the users, libraries have already started using this technology to keep them up to date with the latest happening in chosen websites. It enables users to have customized personal pages that contain contents of various other websites, which would of their use.

IN NUTSHELL

Application of Web 2.0 in libraries has taken the libraries into next generation. Library 2.0 is completely user centric, which provokes libraries to share the resources collectively. It is important for the librarians to experience Web 2.0 tools from a user's perspective and use these tools in modernizing library services. Therefore, librarians have to techno-savvy in today's world of information.

PORTAL

A portal is a site on the World Wide Web that typically provides personalized capabilities to its visitors, providing a pathway to other content. It is designed to use distributed applications, different numbers and types of middleware and hardware to provide services from a number of different sources. In addition, business portals are designed to share collaboration in workplaces. A further business-driven requirement of portals is that the content be able to work on multiple platforms such as personal computers, personal digital assistants (PDAs), and cell phones.

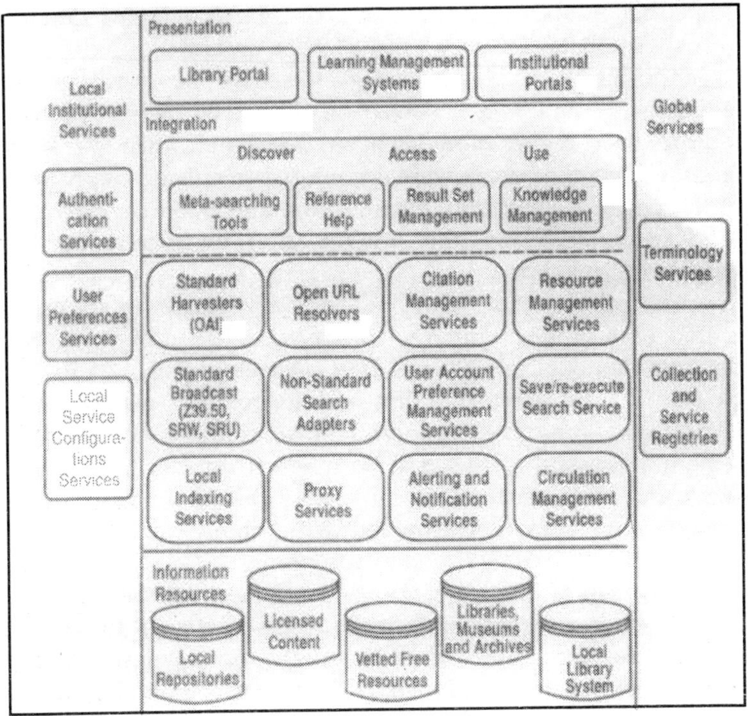

Example : http://library.iisc.ernet.in/
http://www.ncsi.iisc.ernet.in/disc/
http://www.icast.org.in/

DEVELOPMENT OF WEB PORTALS

In the late 1990s, the Web portal was a hot commodity. After the proliferation off Web browsers in the mid-1990s, many companies tried to build or acquire a portal, to have a piece of the Internet market. The Web portal gained special attention because it was, for many users, the starting point of their Web browser. Netscape became a part of America Online, the Walt Disney Company launched Go.com, and Excite became a part of AT&T during the late 1990s. Lycos was said to be a good target for other media companies such as CBS.

Many of the portals started initially as either web directories (notably Yahoo!) and/or search engines (Excite, Lycos, AltaVista, infoseek, and Hotbot among the old ones). Expanding services was a strategy to secure the user-base and lengthen the time a user stayed on the portal. Services which require user registration such as free email, customization features, and chatrooms were considered to enhance repeat use of the portal. Game, chat, email, news, and other services also tend to make users stay longer, thereby increasing the advertising revenue.

The portal craze, with "old media" companies racing to outbid each other for Internet properties, died down with the dot-com flameout in 2000 and 2001. Disney pulled the plug on Go.com, Excite went bankrupt and its remains were sold to iWon.com. Some notable portal sites, for instance, Yahoo!, remain successful to this day. To modern dot-com businesses, the portal craze serves as a cautionary tale about the risks of rushing into a market crowded with highly-capitalized but largely undifferentiated me-too companies.

Because of the continuing expansion of the internet, future web portals that find large success may need to provide portals that access the whole internet, and not just a single media company or conglomerate's internet content. Beginning in 2003, websites like ifoyer.com began using this approach to provide users with portals that attempt to provide internet access from the top down.

REGIONAL WEB PORTALS

Along with the development and success of international Web portals such as Yahoo!, regional variants have also sprung up. Some regional portals contain local information such as weather forecasts, street maps and local business information. Another notable expansion over the past couple of years is the move into formerly unthinkable markets.

"Local content—global reach" portals have emerged not only from countries like India (Rediff), (MswPower.Com), China (Sina.com) and Italy (Webplace.it), but in countries like

Vietnam where they are very important for learning how to apply e-commerce, e-govement, etc. Such portals reach out to the widespread diaspora across the world.

GOVERNMENT WEB PORTALS

At the end of the dot-com boom in the 1990s, many governments had already committed to creating portal sites for their citizens. In the United States the main portal is First Gov.gov; in the United Kingdom the main portals are Directgov (for citizens) and businesslink.gov.uk (for businesses).

Many U.S. states have their own portals which provide direct access to eCommerce applications (e.g., Hawaii Business Express and my Indiana License), agency and department web sites, and more specific information about living in, doing business in and getting around the state.

Many U.S. states have chosen to out-source the operation of their portals to third-party vendors. The most successful company to date for this is NICUSA which runs 18 state portals. NICUSA focuses on the self-funded model, and does not charge the state for work. Instead it is supported by transaction fees for its applications.

CORPORATE WEB PORTALS

Corporate intranets gained popularity during the 1990's. Having access to a variety of company information via a web browser was a new way of working. Intranets quickly grew in size and complexity, and webmasters (many of whom lacked the discipline of managing content and users) became overwhelmed in their duties. It wasn't enough to have a consolidated view of company information, users were demanding personalization and customization. Webmasters, if skilled enough, were able to offer some capabilities, but for the most part ended up driving users away using the intranet.

The 1990's were a time of innovation for the concept of corporate web portals. Many companies began to offer tools to help webmasters manage their data, applications and information more easily, and through personalized views.

Some portal solutions today are able to integrate legacy applications, other portals objects, and handle thousands of user requests.

Today's corporate portals are sprouting new value-added capabilities for businesses. Capabilities such as managing workflows, increasing collaboration between work groups, and allowing content creators to self-publish their information are lifting the burden off already strapped IT departments. In addition, most portal solutions today, if architected correctly, can allow internal and external access to specific corporate information using secure authentication or Single-Sign-On.

JSR168 Standards emerged around 2001. Java Specification Request (JSR) 168 standards allow the interoperability of portlets across different portal platforms. These standards allow portal developers, administrators and consumers to integrate standards-based portals and portlets across a variety of vendor solutions.

HOSTED WEB PORTALS

As corporate portals gained popularity a number of companies began offering them as a hosted service. The hosted portal market fundamentally changed the composition of portals. In many ways they served simply as a tool for publishing information instead of the loftier goals of integrating legacy applications or presenting correlated data from distributed databases. The early hosted portal companies such as Hyperoffice.com, Intranets.com, or the now defunct InternetPortal.com focused on collaboration and scheduling in addition to the distribution of corporate data. As hosted web portals have risen in popularity their feature set has grown to include hosted databases, document management, email, discussion forums and more. Hosted portals automatically personalize the content generated from their modules to provide a personalized experience to their users. In this regard they have remained true to the original goals of the earlier corporate web portals.

ENTERTAINMENT PORTALS

Often all members of an entertainment portal are responsible for its content and direct the type of entertainment that is available to visitors to the site. An example of one such portal is the South African Music and Entertainment portal Overtone These can be an essential part of community-based networking and collaboration.

ENVIRONMENTAL PORTALS

In recent years, many Environmental Portals have been developed in order to raise awareness about Environmental Indicators. Such an example is the EUSOILS (European Soil Portal).

INVESTMENT PORTALS

Investment Portals are an excellent resource when researching global and industry specific markets. An example is InvestorIdeas.com.

MINI PORTALS

Some localized portals are based on local interests, and edited and maintained by individuals. While they do not provide the same levels of services as major portals, they are a good place for collaboration of ideas, for commonly interested people Some examples of mini-portals are KNET at www.silvernet.bravehost.com, and Xbox.net.

VOICE PORTALS

In addition to standard web "sites" accessed through web "browsers", people can also access voice "sites" through voice "browsers". Destinations accessed in this way by Shones are often called Voice Portals.

OPEN ACCESS JOURNAL

At the end of the last century, the combination of powerful desktop computers with electronic distribution over the Internet, prepared the ground for the development of all electronic scientific journals. Today, authors routinely produce what is effectively "camera-ready copy". The rest of the production process is carried out within an all electronic publication system, and the final distribution is on the world-wide-web. Authors and referees generally carry out their work at no charge. These facts provided the stimulus for scientists and institutions to reassess the traditional subscription model of scientific publishing and to come up with a new model appropriate for the digital age; this model has been called Open Access. In 2002 the Budapest Open Access Initiative was the first major international statement to support Open Access. The Bethesda Statement on Open Access Publishing and the Berlin Declaration on Open Access to Knowledge in the Sciences and Humanities followed in 2003. An Open Access publication is one that meets the following two conditions (see Bethesda Statement on Open Access Publishing):

- The author(s) and copyright holder(s) grant(s) to all users a free, irrevocable, worldwide, perpetual right of access to, and a license to copy, use, distribute, transmit and display the work publicly and to make and distribute derivative works, in any digital medium for any responsible purpose, subject to proper attribution of authorship, as well as the right to make small numbers of printed copies for their personal use.
- A complete version of the work and all supplemental materials, including a copy of the permission as stated above, in a suitable standard electronic format is deposited immediately upon initial publication in at least one online repository that is supported by an academic institution, scholarly society, government agency, or other well-established organization that seeks to enable Open Access, unrestricted distribution, interoperability, and long-term archiving

(for the biomedical sciences, PubMed Central is such a repository).

There are two complementary strategies to achieve Open Access to scholarly journal literature (see Budapest Open Access Initiative):

- **Self-archiving:** In addition to publication in a scholarly journal, the article is deposited by the author in an institutional or central repository. Because of copyright restrictions, it is often not possible for the author to deposit the published article itself in these repositories immediately after publication. As a result many archives contain so-called preprints, which means that the deposited article is the initial form, prior to peer-review. Peer reviewed articles, as published in journals, can generally be deposited in repositories at the earliest 6 or 12 month after publication.
- **Open Access journals:** Authors who publish an article in an Open Access journal retain copyright of their work and the articles are available free of charge for all readers immediately upon publication. Additionally, the articles are archived in public repositories, which ensures authors worldwide visibility and impact. Many Open Access journals use an "author pays" business model, whereby authors have to pay the publication costs upfront to make the article available to readers worldwide. In organic chemistry the Beilstein Journal of Organic Chemistry is the only Open Access Journal which is free of charge for both authors and readers. The complete publication costs are met by the Beilstein-Institute. This business model makes the *Beilstein Journal of Organic Chemistry* unique under Open Access journals in organic chemistry.

ISDN: INTEGRATED SERVICES DIGITAL NETWORKS

ISDN is the most important and well planned

development in the field of telecommunications. Integrated services Digital Network (ISDN) is an integrated digital network in which same digital-switches and digital paths are used to establish different services, for example, telephony and data transfer.

The ISDN is an intelligent system for purpose of providing service features, maintenance and network designed for any specific service. It provides end-to-end digital connectivity to support a wide range of service and the digitization process begins right at the user premises. It is possible to support every conceivable service on ISDN. Such service is either a voice or non-voice service. A small set of carefully chosen interfaces enable to support all possible service.

MOTIVATION OF ISDN

Three factors are responsible for the developments towards ISDN:

- Sociological or societal needs
- Economic necessities
- Technological developments

Sociological or Societal Needs

The rapid developments in various facets of society call for increasing and complex communication facilities for example, a senior executive of a company. Who often takes important decision at home late in the evening or while on a holiday, would like to give instant effect to his decisions. Thus may call for access to different computers systems connected in the form a network, electronic banking facilities, facsimile transmission and desktop image processing facilities, all in the place where he is at desktop image processing facilities, all in the place where he is at present. The society is looking for a telecommunication infrastructure that can carry voice, data, image, graphics, video, etc. supported by sophisticated signaling systems. Thus the sociological needs or demand is one of the factors responsible for the development of ISDN.

Economic Necessities

Network provides have to put up separate and independent networks to support different services. Independent networks call for separate administration. Maintenance staff and building for housing switching systems. The independent and duplicate infrastructural facilities lead to high capital cost. Low maintenance efficiency and high management cost. In addition, the network facilities are never fully utilised as the services are independently supported on different networks. The net result is that the overheads turn out to be excessive, leading to become economically unviable network where many different services may be integrated and supported on common network resources, resulted in the development of ISDN.

Technological Development

Searching for new solutions are of no use, unless technology developments make possible such solutions. Earlier, it is the technology factor that brought about the independent network and the end equipments for different services were analog in nature and had different electrical, electronic, sign and communication characteristics. It was necessary to design different network to suit each of these devices.

The desire of the network provides to use a common network infrastructure can be fruitful only if there are uniform electrical signal and communication requirements for all types or services, Such a common requirements (electrical, signal and communication) are provided by the digital technology. Today the digital technology has matured to a level where all the functions of a telecommunication can be achieved in the digital field.

As the name itself suggests, ISDN is the telecommunication network in which all network functions are handled in digital field and a single network will support a set of integrated services.

ISDN will also support the following list of important services:

- Videotext
- Electronic Mail
- Digital Facsimile
- Tele text
- Database access
- Electronic fund transfer
- Image and graphics exchange
- Document storage and transfer
- Automatic alarm services (e.g. Smoke, Fire, Police & Medical)

8

Library and Information Networks

The explosion in the amount of literature that is available, increases among the number of users and their different needs, and the application of electronic media are forcing libraries to construct and participate in networks. Magnetic tapes, floppy disks, and CD-ROMs provide enough data storage capacity. Retrieval through telecommunications networks and access to international databases are available for searching for information on various subjects. With the advent of networks, remote transmission of texts and graphics, video clips and animated clips are also possible.

DEFINITIONS

- A library network is broadly described as a group of libraries coming together with some agreement of understanding to help each other with a view to satisfying the information needs of their clientele.
- UNISIST II working document defines Information Network as a set of inter-related information systems

associated with communication facilities, which are cooperating through more or less formal agreements in order to implement information handling operations to offer better services to the users.

- The National Commission on Libraries and Information Science in its National Programme Document (1975) defines a network as;

Two or more libraries engaged in a common pattern of information exchange, through communications for some functional purpose.

OBJECTIVES

- To promote and support adoption of standards in library operations.
- To create databases for projects, specialists and institutions to provide online information services.
- To improve the efficiency of housekeeping operations.
- To coordinate with other regional, national and international network for exchange of information and documents.
- To generate new services and to improve the efficiency of existing ones.

NETWORK DEVELOPMENT IN INDIA

Some factors that are responsible for the development of library and information networks in India are:

- The report of the working group of the planning commission on modernization of library services and informatics for the Seventh Five Year Plan, 1985-90.
- The National Policy on Library & Information systems document (1986) accepted by the ministry of HRD, Government of India.
- The report on national policy on university libraries prepared by the Association of Indian Universities (1987).

- The UGC report on information systems for science and technology under the Department of Science & Industrial Research (DSIR) Government of India has been vigorously promoting an integrated approach to library automation and networking.

Limitations in Network Development

A network may fail in the early stages if there is not proper planning or if adequate funds are not available. Moreover, a common memorandum of agreement signed by the participating libraries at the institutional level is essential for the success of a network venture. On a more practical level, catalog data must be in a standard, machine readable form for it to be shared and exchanged. And, finally, a continuous flow of external assistance is crucial for the network's survival.

OCLC (ONLINE COMPUTER LIBRARY CENTER)

The OCLC Online Computer Library Center is, according to its website, a "nonprofit, membership, computer library service and research organization dedicated to the public purpose of furthering access to the world's information and reducing information costs". Founded in 1967 as the Ohio College Library Center, more than 60,000 libraries in 112 countries and territories around the world use OCLC services to locate, acquire, catalog, lend and preserve library materials. The organization was founded by Fred Kilgour, and its offices are located in Dublin, Ohio.

OCLC acquired NetLibrary, the largest eContent provider, in 2002 and owns 100% of the shares of OCLC PICA, a library automation systems and services company, which has its headquarters in Leiden in the Netherlands, which was renamed into "OCLC" at the end of 2007. In June 2006, the Research Libraries Group (RLG) merged into OCLC.

Founded in 1967, OCLC Online Computer Library Center is a non-profit, membership, computer library service and research organization dedicated to the public purposes of furthering access to the world's information and reducing the rate of rise of library costs. More than 60,000 libraries in 112 countries and territories around the world use OCLC services to locate, acquire, catalog, lend and preserve library materials.

Researchers, students, faculty, scholars, professional librarians and other information seekers use OCLC services to obtain bibliographic, abstract and full-text information when and where they need it.

OCLC and its member libraries cooperatively produce and maintain WorldCat—the OCLC Online Union Catalog.

MEMBERSHIP

Membership in OCLC is a unique cooperative venture, giving your library access to a wide range of services and databases, including WorldCat. Together OCLC member libraries make up the world's largest consortium.

EXPANDING BEYOND OHIO

In 1977, the Ohio members of OCLC adopted changes in the governance structure that enabled libraries outside Ohio to become members and participate in the election of the Board of Trustees; the Ohio College Library Center became OCLC, Inc. In 1981, the legal name of the corporation became OCLC Online Computer Library Center, Inc. Today, OCLC serves more than 60,000 libraries of all types in the U.S. and 112 countries and territories around the world.

Mission

Connecting people to knowledge through library cooperation.

Vision

The world's libraries. Connected.

Quality Policy

OCLC will continually improve the processes used to deliver its products and services to achieve the OCLC Vision.

How it Works?

Researchers, students, faculty, scholars, professional librarians and other information seekers use OCLC services to obtain bibliographic, abstract and full-text information when and where they need it.

OCLC and its member libraries cooperatively produce and maintain WorldCat—the OCLC Online Union Catalog, the largest Online Public Access Catalog (OPAC) in the world. WorldCat contains holding records from most public and private libraries worldwide. WorldCat is available through many libraries and university computer networks.

The Open WorldCat program makes records of library-owned materials in OCLC's WorldCat database available to Web users on popular Internet search, bibliographic and bookselling sites. OCLC member libraries' catalogs are more accessible from the sites where many people start their search for information.

Open WorldCat records may be accessed through Google or Yahoo's advanced search features, by simply limiting the scope of a search to the site or domain "worldcatlibraries.org." In the fall of 2004, the Open WorldCat collection was expanded to include information about all WorldCat records.

In October 2005, the OCLC technical staff began a wiki-like project that allows readers and librarians to add commentary, and structured-field information, associated with any WorldCat record.

OCLC owns a preservation microfilm and digitization operation called the OCLC Preservation Service Center, with its principal office in Bethlehem, Pennsylvania. Libraries, museums, historical societies, colleges and universities utilize the OCLC Preservation Services to preserve printed works, books, maps, manuscripts, newspapers, etc. in microfilm format for future generations due to its 500-year life expectancy. In addition OCLC Preservation Services converts print and microfilm to digital objects for computer access online database.

OCLC maintains a database for cataloging and searching purposes which is used by librarians and the public. OCLC Passport was one of the computer programs used. Connexion was introduced in 2001 and replaced Passport when it was phased out in May of 2005.

This database contains records in MAchine Readable Cataloging (MARC) format contributed by library catalogers worldwide who use OCLC as a cataloging tool. These MARC format records are then downloaded into the libraries local catalog systems to drive their online catalogs. This allows libraries worldwide to find and download records for materials they want to add to their local catalog without having to go through the lengthy process of cataloging them each individually.

As of February 2007, their database contains over 1.1 billion cataloged items. It remains the world's largest bibliographic database. Connexion is available to professional librarians both as a computer program or on the web at connexion.oclc.org.

WorldCat is also available to the public for searching through a web-based service called FirstSearch, as well as through the Open WorldCat program.

CALIBNET

http://lislinks.ning.com/group/calibnet

Title	:	Calcutta Libraries Network
Sponsor	:	NISSAT—Govt. of India
Applications	:	Cataloging; serials control; acquisitions; circulation

Services: CAS; SDI; union catalog; partial database; editing and retrieval of records; global information; search; full-text document delivery; library automation; CALIBNET INFO Services.

This network links 38 science and technology libraries in the Calcutta metropolitan area. The plan focuses on the introduction of automated systems into the participating libraries before networking them. Each library will have to automate its book acquisition, cataloguing, serials control, fund accounting, and circulation control. Libraries participating in the CALIBNET will use AACR–2 for bibliographic description.

The MAITRAYEE software, which supports MARC records, will enable records to be imported/exported through the CCF. CALIBNET will be linked to DELNET via dial–up access, and to external networks through the GPSS.

BONET

Title	:	Bombay Library Network
Sponsor	:	NISSAT & NCST (1994)
Objective	:	To promote cooperation among libraries in Bombay
Services	:	online catalog; online document delivery; IRS; interlibrary loan; dissemination of information.

BONET was inaugurated on 6 November 1992 at the National Centre for Software Technology (NCST), Bombay. BONET is the latest project sponsored by NISSAT. The network has the following objectives:

- to promote cooperation among libraries in Bombay with emphasis on interlibrary activities rather than computerizing individual libraries;
- to impart training related to library computerization and the networking of Bombay libraries; and
- to build a low cost library information system which can possibly be used as a model for future expansion of this service even outside Bombay.

This is just the beginning. In the years to come many libraries will be automated and linked to a network. This will result in reducing the expenditure incurred in purchasing journals, research materials, etc., and it will improve access to information .

DELNET

Title	:	Developing Library Network
Sponsor	:	NISSAT & NIC (1988)

Objective	:	To promote resource sharing; develop a network of libraries; collect, store, disseminate information
Members	:	165 Institutions, 600 Libraries, 15 States in India, 5 from outside India
Services	:	resource sharing; free Software; ICE online facility; books database; thesis database; Indian specialists; database.

DELNET has been in operation since January 1988 and was registered as a society in 1992. It was initially sponsored by the National Information System for Science and Technology (NISSAT), Department of Scientific and Industrial Research, Government of India and is currently being promoted by the National Informatics Centre, Department of Information Technology, Ministry of Communications and Information Technology, Government of India and India International Centre, New Delhi.

DELNET has been established with the prime objective of promoting *resource sharing* among the libraries through the development of a network of libraries. It aims to collect, store, and disseminate information besides offering computerised services to users, to coordinate efforts for suitable collection development and also to reduce unnecessary duplication wherever possible.

DELNET has been actively engaged with the compilation of various Union Catalogues of the resources available in member-libraries. It has already created the Union Catalogue of Books, Union List of Current Periodicals, Union Catalogue of Periodicals, D-ROM Database, Database of Indian Specialists, Database of Periodical Articles, Union List of Video Recordings, Urdu Manuscripts' Database, Database of Theses and Dissertations, DEVINSA Database, sample databases of language publications using GIST technology and several other databases. The data is being updated in each of these databases and is growing rapidly. All the DELNET databases have been resident on DELSIS, in-house software developed on BASISPlus, an RDBMS, the product of Information Dimensions Inc. of USA which has been provided to DELNET courtesy National Informatics Centre, New Delhi.

DELNET provides an array of facilities including E-mail to its member-libraries including both institutional and associate institutional members. DELNET'S relentless efforts in resource sharing have proved extremely effective. It has indeed been a big leap towards the modernisation of libraries in India.

THE MAIN OBJECTIVES OF DELNET

- To promote sharing of resources among the libraries by developing a network of libraries, by collecting, storing and disseminating information and by offering computerised services to the users;
- To undertake scientific research in the area of Information Science and Technology, create new systems in the field, apply the results of research and publish them;
- To offer technical guidance to the member-libraries on collecting, storing, sharing and disseminating information;
- To coordinate efforts for suitable collection development and reduce unnecessary duplication wherever possible;
- To establish/facilitate the establishment of referral and/or research centres, and maintain a central online union catalogue of books, serials and non-book materials of all the participating libraries;
- To facilitate and promote delivery of documents manually or mechanically;
- To develop specialised bibliographic database of books, serials and non-book materials;
- To develop databases of projects, specialists and institutions;
- To possess and maintain electronic and mechanical equipment for speedy communication of information and delivery of electronic mail; and
- To coordinate with other regional, national and international networks and libraries for exchange of information and documents.

ADINET

Title	:	Ahmedabad Library Network
Sponsor	:	NISSAT, DSIR (1994) & INFLIBNET
Objective	:	To bring cooperation among its regional libraries; to develop data bases; to integrate scientific and technical information systems
Members	:	Nine libraries
Services	:	Library automation; library holdings; database in progress

MYLIBNET

Title	:	Mysore Library Network
Sponsor	:	NISSAT (1994)
Objective	:	Developing software tools; conducting seminar; workshops/training programs; conduct surveys
Host Site	:	CFTRI, Mysore
Members	:	116 Institutions
Services	:	MYLIB Database; E-journals; food patents; CFTRI Library Bulletin; public services.

BALNET

Title	:	Bangalore Library Network
Sponsor	:	JRD Tata Memorial Library (1995)
Members	:	100 Libraries

MALIBNET

Title	:	Madras Library Network
Sponsor	:	INSDOC & NISSAT (1993)
Members	:	15 Libraries
Activity	:	Two important databases, a directory database of current serials in Madras and a contents database covering articles published in 300 journals available in Madras libraries.

MALIBNET—a registered society (non-government organisation) was formed in 1993.Through an MOU, Indian National Scientific Documentation Center (INSDOC) has been entrusted the responsibility of setting up and provides technical support for operating the network. Presently, nearly 50 libraries in Madras are contributing actively to the creation of various databases on Malibnet. With the help of communication links and sophisticated information technology, the resources of the member libraries are shared and made available to the users. Presently 17 major educational/research institutions have joined as member institutions of MALIBNET.

INFLIBNET

Title	:	Information Library Network
Sponsor	:	UGC (1991)
Connectivity	:	Computer communication network of universities and R&D; libraries and bibliographic information centers throughout the country Members 200 Universities; 400 College libraries; 200 R&D libraries
Services	:	Catalog service; database Services; document supply services; e-mail; BBS: audio and video conferencing, etc.

Information and Library Network (INFLIBNET) Centre is an autonomous Inter-University Centre of the University Grants Commission (UGC) of India. It is a major National Programme initiated by the UGC in 1991 with its Head Quarters at Gujarat University Campus, Ahmedabad. Initially started as a project under the IUCAA, it became an independent Inter-University Centre in 1996.

INFLIBNET is involved in modernizing university libraries in India and connecting them as well as information centres in the country through a nation-wide high speed data network using the state-of-art technologies for the optimum utilisation of information. INFLIBNET is set out to be a major player in promoting scholarly communication among academicians and researchers in India.

The Primary Objectives of INFLIBNET as Envisaged in Memorandum of Association

- To promote and establish communication facilities to improve capability in information transfer and access, that provide support to scholarship, learning, research and academic pursuit through cooperation and involvement of agencies concerned.
- Communication network for linking libraries and information centres in universities, deemed to be universities, colleges, UGC information centres, institutions of national importance and R & D institutions, etc. avoiding duplication of efforts.

FUNCTIONS

In order to fulfil the broad objectives, INFLIBNET will do the following:

- Promote and implement computerisation of operations and services in the libraries and information centres of the country, following a uniform standard.
- Evolve standards and uniform guidelines in techniques, methods, procedures, computer hardware and software, services and promote their adoption in actual practice by all libraries, in order to facilitate pooling, sharing and exchange of information towards optimal use of resources and facilities.
- Evolve a national network interconnecting various libraries and information centers in the country and to improve capability in information handling and service.
- Provide reliable access to document collection of libraries by creating on-line union catalogue of serials, theses/dissertations, books, monographs and non-book materials (manuscripts, audio-visuals, computer data, multimedia, etc.) in various libraries in India.

- Provide access to bibliographic information sources with citations, abstracts, etc. through indigenously created databases of the Sectoral Information Centers of NISSAT, UGC Information Centre's, City Networks and such others and by establishing gateways for on-line accessing of national and international databases held by national and international information networks and centres respectively.
- Develop new methods and techniques for archival of valuable information available as manuscripts and information documents in different Indian Languages, in the form of digital images using high density storage media.
- Optimise information resource utilization through shared cataloguing, inter-library loan service, catalogue production, collection development and thus avoiding duplication in acquisition to the extent possible.
- Enable the users dispersed all over the country, irrespective of location and distance, to have access to information regarding serials, theses/dissertations, books, monographs and non-book materials by locating the sources wherefrom available and to obtain it through the facilities of INFLIBNET and union catalogue of documents.
- Create databases of projects, institutions, specialists, etc. for providing on-line information service.
- Encourage co-operation among libraries, documentation centres and information centres in the country, so that the resources can be pooled for the benefit of helping the weaker resource centres by stronger ones.
- Train and develop human resources in the field of computerised library operations and networking to establish, manage and sustain INFLIBNET.
- Facilitate academic communication amongst scientists, engineers, social scientists, academics, faculties, researchers and students through electronic

mail, file transfer, computer/audio/video conferencing, etc.

- Undertake system design and studies in the field of communications, computer networking, information handling and data management.
- Establish appropriate control and monitoring system for the communication network and organise maintenance.
- Collaborate with institutions, libraries, information centres and other organisations in India and abroad in the field relevant to the objectives of the Centre.
- Create and promote R&D and other facilities and technical positions for realising the objectives of the Centre.
- Generate revenue by providing consultancies and information services.

MEMBERSHIP

1. Primary Membership

The University Libraries entitled to receive grants from UGC will become primary members immediately on receipt of the initial grant under the INFLIBNET programme. The responsibility and benefit of primary membership are mentioned in Memorandam of Understanding (MOU) which is signed by the member Library with INFLIBNET.

2. Associate Membership : [Under Consideration]

The Libraries who are not entitled to receive the grants from the UGC but are public funded academic and research organisation, Government department, Non-profit making organisation can become the associate membership of INFLIBNET by signing an MOU and by paying the requisite fees. The details are given in MOU.

INFONET

The UGC-Infonet E-journal consortium is our pride in the field of education and research which has been formally launched on the concluding day of UGC's Golden Jubilee celebrations by his Excellency the *President of India, Dr. A.P.J. Abdul Kalam* at Vigyan Bhawan on 28th December 2003 by dedicating a bouquet of e-journals to the nation.

With globalization of education and competitive research the demand for the journals has increased over the years. Due to scarcity of funds, libraries have been forced to discontinue the scholarly journals, which have great impact to the users. In order to provide the current literature to academia, UGC has initiated the UGC-INFONET: E-journal consortium. Timely initiative of UGC is a great boon to academia in the country, which enables them to access large number of scholarly journals from reputed publishers, aggregators and society publications. Under the consortium, about 4000 full text scholarly electronic journals from 25 publishers across the globe can be accessed. The consortium provides current as well as archival access to core and peer-reviewed journals in different disciplines. The whole programme has been implemented in different phases. So far 100 Universities out of 171 Indian Universities, which come under the purview of UGC, have been provided access to these journals and it will gradually be extended to affiliated colleges as well. It covers almost all areas of learning like Arts, Humanities, Social Sciences, Physical and Chemical Sciences, Life Sciences, Computer Sciences, Mathematics and Statistics, etc. and other subject areas are to be added in near future. The programme is wholly funded by the UGC and monitored by INFLIBNET (Information and Library Network) Centre, Ahmedabad.

9 General Networks in India

NICNET

http://home.nic.in/

Title	:	National Information Center Network.
Sponsor	:	Planning Commission, Govt. of India.
Membership	:	Four national and regional nodes, 32 state and union territory nodes; seventy cities and towns.
Services	:	Bulk file transfer; teleconferencing; full text and bibliographic retrieval services.
Application	:	ICMRNIC Center; MEDLARS in India; Chemical Abstracts database.

NICNET was established by National Information Centre as an information network in the country. It has primarily been set-up to link various departments of the government for decision optimisation, i.e., to use new technologies of computer networking to ensure a systematic procedure for information exchange between the centre and the states, between and their districts and among various departments/

ministries of the state and Central government as well as between them and the public.

AIMS AND OBJECTIVES

NICNET was established to fulfil the following objectives:

- To design, develop and implement advanced computer based methodology.
- To promote adoption of computer-based management techniques.
- To join internally together through the computer networks to all of the departments, autonomous bodies and organizations of central government of India in the form of a government information system of the country.
- To set-up a computer for connecting the various government departments.
- To generate specialized manpower in the field of information.

ARCHITECTURE

NICNET has more than 250 micro earth stations operating in different parts of the country. It links four regional nodes at Delhi, Pune, Bhubaneshwar and Hyderabad and established 32 nodes at the state and union territories levels and 439 nodes at district headquarters. By this architecture NICNET facilitates the provision of reliable data communication to the government agencies at the place of work. A number of information systems have been established under this network in the areas of accounts, budgets, central excises, import-export distribution, estate duties, etc. It has established District Information System, which is a network, based data bank of NIC for better planning and efficient decision-making about the districts.

SERVICES

Several types of services are being provided through this network. They are as follows:

- **E-mail:** Electronic mail service of NICNET is the value added electronic mail. This service enables all users to transmit and receive mail. This mail service has been custom designed taking into consideration the network architecture and operation environment.
- **Bibliographic Service:** A major bibliographic application that is available on this network is the bibliographic biomedical information. NIC has established ICMR-NIC centers for biomedical information in 1986, which has been providing services to users in the country form MED line, POPline, CHEMBANK and cancer databases. This centre also conducts training courses, workshops and seminars aimed at preparing cadre of biomedical librarians, well versed in the latest information technologies.
- **Electronic Information Service:** Since 1989 NICNET providing this service for 3 Loksabha elections held in the country. NIC has also developed software in C language for poll results processing.

Patent Information System: NIC also developed a computerized online patent information system based on bibliographic data available from the International Patent Documentation Centre (INPADOC), Vienna. This system creates information and multi-valued index directory files which facilitate faster and efficient retrieval of patent documents according to the International Patent Classification Code.

INDONET

http://web.indo.net.id/

Title : INDONET data Network

Sponsor	:	CMC Ltd (1986) = Informatics India Ltd (1989)
Membership	:	Commercial computer network
Services	:	Database services such as DIALOG, COMPUSERVE; IP; SHARP
Applications	:	ACME; file transfer; international gateway

The INDONET is a computer-based network commissioned by CMC (Computer maintenance corporation) Ltd. It comprises a network of computers located in many cities and connected by a data communication links. The first phrase link large sized computer systems located at Bombay, Delhi, Madras, Calcutta, and Hyderabad. The user will have access to the network through terminals located at CMC computer centre or through terminals located remotely and connected to the local computer system through voice grade P&T lines at a speed of 300-1200 b.p.s.

I—NET (VIKRAM)

http://www.ssat-inet.net/

Title	:	I—NET
Sponsor	:	Dept. of Telecommunications, Govt. of India
Connectivity	:	Packet switched public data network covering nine cities
Services	:	Information exchange through e-mail/ FTP; Bibliographic databases.

It is public data network, established by DOT, this network operates on packet switching mode. It supports data communication switching amongst terminals and computers of different speed and protocol. All data switching facilities as per international standards (CCITT) are provided through this network. The network has a potential for several applications for individuals, corporate bodies, computer facilities, banking industry, airlines and transport sector and for telematics services like electronic mail. Videotext, telex, etc.

MYLIBNET

Title	:	Mysore Library Network
Sponsor	:	NISSAT (1994)
Objective	:	Developing software tools; conducting seminar; workshops/training programs; conduct surveys
Host Site	:	CFTRI, Mysore
Members	:	116 Institutions
Services	:	MYLIB Database; E-journals; food patents; CFTRI Library Bulletin; public services.

The MYLIBNET was set-up during May 1995 in the city of Mysore with financial support from NISSAT, and is housed at the Central Food Technological Research Institute. About 116 colleges/institutions are affiliated to the University of Mysore; of these 34 college libraries are located within Mysore. These were networked in the first phase. The objectives of the MYLIBNET are: to share resources of the libraries, to provide e-mail, to develop software tools for better library management, to create awareness in the field of information technology, to set-up an information base in collaboration with industry, to conduct surveys and disseminate information about new arrivals of books/journals and events like seminars/workshops/training programmes. MALIBNET offers such services as assistance to automate library in-house operations, e-mail under ERNET, access to various databases, training of trainers in information technology, and hosting of member library information on the server for the participating libraries.

DESINET

Title	:	Defence Science Information Network
Sponsor	:	DESIDOC, Delhi

Activity	:	Focus on scientific, research and defense communities

DESINET is a proposed bibliographic information network for defence covering only unclassified scientific and technical information. The Defence Science Information Documentation Centre, New Delhi, would take the initiative in planning and implementing the network. The users of DESINET would be scientific, research and defence personnel from the Department of Defence, Department of Defence R&D, and the Department of Defence Production & Supplies. The defence bibliographic information network will also have close links with other similar networks like NICNET for exchange of information on mutually agreed terms.The other networks in the pipeline are Bombay Library Network (BONET) and Hyderabad Library Network (HYLIBNET).

ERNET

Title	:	Educational and Research Network
Sponsor	:	Dept. of Electronics, Govt. of India; UNESCO (Financial assistance from UNDP)
Members	:	Eight institutions (5 IITs, IISc., National Centre for Software Technology—Bombay, CCI wing of Dept. of Electronics)
Services	:	Communication services such as e-mail, file transfer, remote log on, database access, bulletin board, etc.

ERNET (Education and Research Network) has made a significant contribution to the emergence of networking in the country. It practically brought the Internet to India and has built up national capabilities in the area of net-working, especially in protocol software engineering. It has not only succeeded in building a large network that provides various facilities to the intellectual segment of Indian society—the research and education community, it has over the years become a trendsetter in the field of networking. UNDP has lauded ERNET as one of the most successful programmes it has funded. The Govt. of India has committed itself to further strengthen the project by including it in the 9th Plan with the allocation of funds and by creation of a new organisational set-up in the form of a Society. The Science community of the country has also recognized ERNET's contribution—both for infrastructure services as well as for R&D. The Scientific Advisory Committee to the Cabinet has adopted ERNET as the platform for launching an S&T network in the country.

HOW IT BEGAN

ERNET was initiated in 1986 by the Department of Electronics (DoE), with funding support from the Government of India and United Nations Development Program (UNDP), involving eight premier institutions as participating agencies—NCST (National Centre for Software Technology) Bombay, IISc (Indian Institute of Science) Bangalore, five IITs (Indian Institutes of Technology) at Delhi, Bombay, Kanpur, Kharagpur and Madras, and the DoE, New Delhi. ERNET began as a multi protocol network with both the TCP/IP and the OSI-IP protocol stacks running over the leased-line portion of the backbone. Since 1995, however, almost all traffic is carried over TCP/IP.

THE OBJECTIVES OF ERNET INDIA

ERNET operations, i.e. providing state-of-the-art communication infrastructure and services to Academic and Research institutions, Government organisations, NGOs, private sector R&D organisations, and various other non-commercial organisations;

- Research and development;
- Training and Consultancy;
- Content development.

ACHIEVEMENTS

Foundation of National Capability Building in the Area of Computer Networking Laid through

Setting up of a chain of core groups at the participating agencies with a minimal set of lab facilities and creation of skilled manpower to carry out R&D.

- Generating man power at different levels.
- Making the world of standards (TCP/IP, OSI, etc.) well understood.
- Providing an insight into emerging issues such as ATM networks, networked multi-media, and information infrastructure.

Network Infrastructure and Services Set-up, Including

- Installation, maintenance and operation of large Campus LANs.
- Design, commissioning and testing of SATWAN hub and the installation of VSATs.
- Seamless interconnection of LAN-WAN segments, and multi-protocol capability provided.
- Provision of the whole range of Internet services.
- Deployment of TDM/TDMA-based VSAT network for Internet access.

Research and Development

Research and Development in the area of computer networking has been the forte of ERNET.

SIRNET

Title	:	Scientific and Industrial Research Network
Sponsor	:	CSIR (Commissioned Agency—NCST, Bombay)

Members	:	40 labs and R&D Institutions
Applications	:	scientific communication; leather technology; natural products; food technology; medicinal Plants.

The Council of Scientific and Industrial Research set up a computer communication network (SIRNET) for the exchange of information among its 40 or more laboratories during 1990. SIRNET uses the infrastructure of ERNET. The main objective of SIRNET is to help organizing indigenous online database services on leather technology, food technology, natural products, chemistry, radio physics and medicinal plants. It planned to provide a bulletin board service and set up teleconferencing facilities through the network apart from facilitating the flow of routine administrative and financial information and the exchange of library resources.

VIDYANET

Title	:	VIDYANET (Dedicated Communication Computer Net).
Sponsor	:	TATA Institute of Fundamental Research, Bombay.
Objectives	:	To provide rapid means of communications by linking computers at various institutions in India to similar networks outside the country; to stimulate corporate research, the day-to-day exchange of research information and the execution of joint projects and publications.
Services	:	File transfer facility; sharing of computer resources and access to remote applications, databases, libraries, etc.

VIDYANET is a proposed dedicated communication/ computer network to meet the needs of scientists and research workers in laboratories/institutions of excellence in the country. The major objective of the network is to stimulate co-operative research, day-to-day exchange of research information and to execute joint projects and publications. In the first phase VIDYANET would link up ten institutions: the All India Institute of Medical Sciences (New Delhi), the Indian Agricultural Research Institute (New Delhi), the five IITs, the Indian Statistical Institute (Calcutta), the National Physical Laboratory (New Delhi), the Bhabha Atomic Research Centre (Mumbai), the Indian Institute of Geomagnetism (Calcutta), the National Centre for Software Technology (Mumbai) and the Tata Institute of Fundamental Research (Mumbai). Subsequent phases of networking would cover leading institutions in Ahmedabad, Bangalore, Bhopal, Calcutta and Chennai. It aims to link up institutional computers (Cyber, VAX, DEC, etc.) via telecommunication lines and provide facilities like transfer of files of any type ± data, programs and documents, electronic mail, exchange of immediate messages, access to remote applications, databases and libraries. It intends to allow users to develop databases on specialized areas like biotechnology, superconductivity and supernova research. It also aims at providing rapid means of communication by linking computers at various institutions in India and abroad with similar networks like EARN (European Academic Research Network, Geneva) and BITNET through a gateway.

BTISNET (Biotechnology Information System Network)

Title	:	BTISNET (Specialized Information Network).
Sponsor	:	Dept. of Biotechnology, Govt. of India.
Connectivity	:	10 Specialized Information Centres in genetic engineering, plant tissue culture; photosynthesis and plant molecular biology; cell transformation; bio-process engineering.
Services	:	Data processing using applications software; online communication access; facsimile facility.

Research and Development activities in Modern Biology and Biotechnology are very much information-dependent fields. In fact the symbiosis between information technology and Biotechnology today is as intricately entwined as like the two strands of the DNA helix. Various Genome projects including the Human Genome Project (HGP) are producing enormous amounts of Sequences data. The rate of growth of these data has been estimated to be more than 200 million bases per year. The content of the database itself is doubling in size approximately every year. The large amounts of data generated through various forms are serving as a source of knowledge to the scientists engaged in the field of Biotechnology. The whole paradigm shift in molecular biology towards data-intensive research in search of useful genes is basically due to the fact that the genetic data is becoming the major driving force in drug discovery, protein engineering, design of new molecules and other related areas. The impact of Bioinformatics on Indian Biosciences and Biotechnology can be seen both in tangible and non-tangible terms. R&D activities in these fields grew in quantity as well as quality as can be seen from research papers.

PUBLISHED FROM INDIA

INDIAN RAILWAYS RAILNET

The Indian Railways is Asia's largest and the world's second largest rail network. Adopting e-Governance in right earnest and to reap the benefit of IT explosion, Indian Railways have established a 'Corporate Wide Information System' (CWIS) called RAILNET. It provides smooth flow of information on demand for administrative purposes, which would enable taking quicker and better decisions.

Realising the important role that information plays in customer services and in railways operations, IR had embarked on its computerisation program. IR developed a dedicated skeletal communication network, as a basic requirement for train operation. After the early introduction of basic computer applications e.g. Pay rolls, Inventory Control and Operating Statistics, Railways went for deployment of computers for productivity improvement through building up operational databases.

USE OF IT IN RAILWAY

Passenger Reservation System (PRS)

CONCERT (Country-wide Network of Computerised Enhanced Reservation & Ticketing), Indian Railways fully automated PRS software, is a complex online distributed transaction application based on client server architecture interconnecting the regional computing system into a National PRS grid. The salient features of CONCERT software include allowing passenger from anywhere to do a booking for a journey in any train in any class from anywhere to anywhere; handling reservation, modifications cancellation/refunds.

E-TICKETING

CRIS (Centre for Railway Information System) has successfully developed the Internet ticketing solution launched by IRCTC (Indian Railway Catering and Tourism Corporation). The effort involved interfacing the IRCTC front end with backend PRS Alpha servers, writing procedures for search and queries at the backend, ticket printing on existing clients and accounting software.

UTS (UNRESERVED TICKET SYSTEM)

UTS is the complete solution for computerised unreserved ticketing from dedicated counter terminals and replaces manual Printed Card Tickets/Excess Fare Tickets/Blank Paper Tickets. In future, ticketing from handheld terminals smart card, automatic vending machines, etc. is also envisaged.

IVRS (INTERACTIVE VOICE RESPONSE SYSTEM)

IVRS is a telephonic enquiry system which information such as Passenger Name Record (PNR) enquiry, Train Arrival/ Departure information enquiry through NTES, and Berth availability position in any train, in multiple languages.

NTES (NATIONAL TRAIN ENQUIRY SYSTEM)

NTES provides arrival/departure as well as current status information about any passenger train in the entire Indian Railways. NTES is parallel to PRS. The servers are located at five metros, i.e. Delhi, Kolkata, Mumbai, Chennai, Secunderabad and all are interconnected. Entries are made regarding running of train every half an hour at various locations including divisional headquarter all over the Indian Railways. NTES is used by IVRS and other web enabled services and mobile services for providing train information to the public.

Bibliography

Alt, Franz L and Rubinboff, Morrins, ed. Advances in computers.Newyork:Academinc press, 1989.

Dawson, A. The Internet for Library and Information Professionals.London:Library Association Publishing,1997.

Devarajan, G and Rahelamma, A.V ed.Library computerisation in india.New Delhi:Ess Ess Publication,1990.

Eric Hunder, Computerized cataloguing. London: Bingly, 1985.

Implementation of Koha—An Open Source Library Management Software information and knowledge management projects, NCSI IISc, Banglore.

Institutional digital assets managements using digital library. Information and knowledge managements project, NCSI IISc, Banglore.

Iyer,V.K.Library Information Network management. New Delhi:Commonwealth Publishing,1999.

Krishan Gopal.Modern Library Automation. Delhi: Authors Press, 999.

Kumar, P.S.G. Computerization of Indian Libraries. New Delhi: B.R.Pub Corporation, 1977.

Kusum Verma. Ed. Uase of Web in Libraries. New Delhi: Akansha Publishing House, 2004.

Lovecy, Ian. Automating Library Procedures: a survivors handbook. D.K. Publisher (Library Association, London), New Delhi, 1992.

Luck Tedd, Introduction to Computer-based Library System, Hyden, 1977.

Rajiv Adhikari, Library serials Automation, Delhi: Rajat Publication, 2000.

Raman Nair, R., Internet for Information Service. New Delhi: Ess Ess Publications, 2002.

Rao, Ravichandra, I.K., Libray Automation. New Age International Publishers, 2nd ed. (1996).

Reynolds, D., Library Automation: issues and application. New York: Bowker & Co, 1984.

Satyanarayana, N.R., A Manual of Library Automation and Networking. New Royal Book Co., 2003.

Sharma, Pandey, S.K., Library computerisation: Theory & Practice. New Delhi: Ess Ess Publications, 1993.

Tedd, L.A., 1984. An Introduction to Computer-based Library System. 2nd ed., New York, USA: John Wiley & Sons, 1984.

Tenenbaum, Andrew S., Computer network. 2nd ed. Engleword Cliffs, NJP: Prentice Hall, 1988.

Index